David Smith is a solicitor specialising in residential property, agency, and regulatory law. He is a partner at JMW Solicitors LLP in London. He is well known for his work in the residential property and agency field, especially in property licensing and consumer law and has advised local and national governments, large and small landlords and tenants and letting and estate agents across the sector.

Renting Homes: The New Law of Letting in Wales

Renting Homes: The New Law of Letting in Wales

David Stuart Nicholas Smith

Solicitor (England and Wales)

BSc (Econ), LLB, PhD (Wales)

Law Brief Publishing

Published 2023 by Law Brief Publishing, an imprint of Law Brief Publishing Ltd
30 The Parks
Minehead
Somerset
TA24 8BT

www.lawbriefpublishing.com

Paperback: 978-1-913715-49-6

For Dee and Aanya yet again.
With love as always.

PREFACE

For me this book was always inevitable. As a trainee solicitor I co-authored one of the first books on the Housing Act 2004, an earth-shaking piece of legislation for the residential landlord and tenant sector. That book has come to define much of my legal career and the careful analysis of the legislation that it required ended up providing me with skills and experience that have been of great benefit to me throughout. Therefore, when I was first asked to be a special advisor to the Welsh Assembly during the passing of the bill that became the Renting Homes (Wales) Act 2016 it seemed obvious that I would end up writing about the law when it came into effect. I did not expect that I would be doing that writing so very far into the future! My approach to this book, as with so many of my books, was very much guided by my early legal influences, especially the late Professor James Driscoll who I was lucky enough to meet and lecture alongside on several occasions. His influence has even extended to me borrowing the title for this book from his guide to the Housing Act 2004.

This book does not claim to be a complete guide to the Act. It is a comprehensive review of the legislation and its attendance regulations and I have included extensive footnotes to make it possible to see where the commentary relates to the Act. However, while I have tried to bring out some of the existing case law which is likely to be relevant to the Act, I am conscious that there is far more that I have not touched on. Equally, I have glossed over some of the provisions of the Act that I consider to be of less immediate interest. Therefore, this book is at best a detailed overview of a complex new piece of legislation.

As always, while my name appears on the front cover there are a number of other people who deserve substantial credit. My wife is foremost among these as she has again put up with my broken promises not to write any more books for a bit. Professor David Cowan got me involved in Wales in the first place and so bears much of the responsibility for me writing about it at all. Justin Bates was always helpful when I wanted to check I was reading a complex part of the legislation properly. However, none of these people are to blame for any errors in the text, that is entirely my responsibility.

The law is correct as at 10 December 2022.

David Smith
December 2022

CONTENTS

CHAPTER ONE

INTRODUCTION

The Renting Homes (Wales) Act 2016 (RHWA throughout this text) is intended to be a completely new system of housing law in Wales extending to both the private and social housing sectors. It is a part of a larger process of change in Wales which seeks to reconfigure the regulation and control of housing in Wales.

There has been a degree of change already with existing legislation introducing private landlord and agent registration and control over fees charged to tenants. The process has stalled considerably with the RHWA which was passed in 2016 and had found itself languishing for six years before coming into force. The length of the delay is perhaps best illustrated by the fact that it has been modified before coming into force[1] and that there was a consultation in the last two months before the RHWA came into effect[2] leading to further modifications which will lead to further changes coming into force the night before the RHWA came into effect.[3] These further changes illustrate how far the landscape, particularly in the private rented sector, has shifted during the period that the RHWA has been awaiting its implementation. Indeed, the RHWA, which was once considered to be a radical and far-reaching reform has ended up being partially overtaken by developments in the other main UK jurisdictions and the delays in its implementation have actually ended up leaving Wales as the UK jurisdiction with the lowest level of

---

[1] By the Renting Homes (Amendment) (Wales) Act 2021.

[2] See the consultation entitled Renting Homes (Wales) Act 2016: improving security of tenure by increasing the period of notice. Available at https://gov.wales/renting-homes-wales-act-2016-improving-security-tenure-increasing-period-notice.

[3] Made by the Renting Homes (Wales) Act 2016 (Amendment of Schedule 12 and Consequential Amendment) Regulations 2022.

1

tenant protection as other jurisdictions have made changes to increase standards and improve tenant rights.

Nonetheless the changes being made by the RHWA should be seen in the wider context of Wales seeking to take control of its legal system. In that sense making the fullest use of devolved powers to do something different to the other part of the UK is an important part of the development of a distinct Welsh legal identity. In addition, Wales has bravely grasped the nettle of housing reform and, rather than making small alterations at the edges as England has done, has elected to attempt a root and branch reform of both the private and social sectors in an effort to bring them into the similar legal structure. That effort, even if it is not successful, is one that should be respected even if it ultimately fails in that it seeks to simplify an increasingly complex legal structure replacing it with something, which while still complicated, brings a range of obligations into a single piece of legislation.

CHAPTER TWO

LAW IN WALES

One of the challenges when looking at the new housing law in Wales is interpretation of uncertain provisions. There are several issues that coincide to make this difficult.

First, there is the problem of size. Wales is a smaller jurisdiction. By no means the smallest one in the UK, but still smaller than England. The PRS is also fairly small so there is a more limited pool from which cases can be drawn and there is always going to be a reluctance on the part of private landlords to incur the costs of an appeal when there is frequently an alternative route to achieve their objective, which is usually eviction. In the past, this was less of an issue in Wales as England had the same legislative provisions and so they could rely on English cases as well to clarify provisions. Of course, as Wales diversifies from England this benefit evaporates and Wales must either generate its own cases on appeal or live with the uncertainty. This problem is exacerbated in the housing sector by the small number of Welsh practitioners in this area and the significant chunks of Wales that suffer from little or no legal assistance, especially for those with little ability to pay.

The other principal difficulty with the development of Welsh law through the courts is that Wales must share a court system with England. While some Welsh legislation makes use of the Welsh tribunals, they are actually less used than those in England and are largely peripheral to the enforcement of Welsh law. There has been little movement to use the tribunals more fully, as there has been in Scotland. Therefore changes in Welsh housing law have not being reflected well in changing court procedures and some of the delays in making changes in Wales appear to have occurred as a result of difficulties in negotiations with the Ministry of Justice and HM Courts and Tribunals Service. Wales also suffers from the problem that, where it shares legislation with England, the courts can effectively make changes to Welsh legislation, or at least change how it is interpreted, where they are ruling on English cases. In one sense this is how it has always been. But where Welsh law is devolved, and it is trying to do its own thing, this becomes more of a problem.

There is also a difficulty for the Welsh Government in terms of taking part in English legislation. To join into an English piece of legislation the Senedd must pass a Legislative Consent Motion ("LCM"). LCMs are based on an October 2013 Memorandum of Understanding between UK Government and the Ministers of the various devolved bodies.[4] However, in practice LCMs need to happen early in a Bill if the devolved body wants to have much say in the shaping of the Bill involved. This can be very hard where time is short. For example, the Coronavirus Act 2020 was first read in Parliament on 19 March 2020, the second reading was on 23 March 2020 and it went through its committee stages that day before having the third reading the same evening. The Senedd passed its LCM on 24 March 2020, the same day the Bill went to the House of Lords, and had many of its initial stages there. While this is an extreme example the reality is that LCMs often do not happen simply because the Senedd is brought in too late to have much hope of shaping the Bill and therefore prefers to do its own thing.

Second, there is the issue of the use of guidance. Wales has tended to use guidance far more than other UK jurisdictions. This guidance has statutory underpinning in that Welsh legislation frequently allows for Welsh ministers to issue guidance which local authorities in Wales are required to have regard to. In some cases, this guidance is absolutely required to be issued[5] in other cases the guidance is optional but if it is issued it must be followed.[6] This allows for a high level of flexibility as

---

[4] Available at https://www.gov.uk/government/uploads/system/uploads/attachment_data/file/316157/MoU_between_the_UK_and_the_Devolved_Administrations.pdf.

[5] For example, s40, Housing (Wales) Act 2014.

[6] For example, s15, Renting Homes (Fees etc.) (Wales) Act 2019.

the guidance can be quickly altered. However, it also means that there is difficulty challenging the approach of ministers as the only way to do so is to pursue a judicial review, an expensive and risky undertaking.

Third, there is the difficulty of understanding what the Senedd Cymru intended. Legislation in the Welsh Assembly is often introduced with fairly brief statements from the government and is frequently subject to substantial amendment at very late stages in the Bill process. As such, there has tended to be little oversight of the final versions of Bills before they are passed into law. This has been exacerbated by a tendency to place a great deal of power into the hands of Welsh Ministers by giving them extensive powers to pass statutory instruments which dictate the structure of key pieces of legislation. As an extreme example the consequential repeals and amendments relating to the RHWA are not on the face of the Act and are set out in a Statutory Instrument. This has led to considerable uncertainty as to the scope of the RHWA. Additionally, the Senedd has a surprisingly limited degree of public debate about the text of Bills from which their intention can be divined. This is exacerbated by the partial use of proportional representation which encourages members to display strong party loyalty in order to protect their place on the party list element of the election process. The same problem occurs in the committee stages of Bills where the Welsh government is not often required to fully explain its intent and privately agrees with Members to amend Bills so that committee reports have no substantive discussion or criticism in them of the Bill as the points have already been resolved. While this is undoubtedly good for elected representatives it is difficult for the courts who are seeking to understand what it was that the Senedd might truly might have intended by a particular provision.[7]

Finally, the structure of Welsh legislation is itself problematic. The Welsh government has adopted a drafting style which is common within the EU by trying to set out in its Bills what each forthcoming section is trying to

---

[7] Some comment on these issues can be found in *Jarvis v Evans* [2020] EWCA Civ 854 @ 42(vi).

achieve. This makes sense from the perspective of readability in that it is not necessary to read every provision to get a good idea of what the relevant legislation is trying to do and where each of those objectives is made flesh. However, from the point of view of the courts this creates a very serious issue. Should overview sections be interpreted as merely setting out what is to come in the sections to follow? If so, this make statutory interpretation harder as these sections are, from a legal perspective, nugatory, and the courts dislike assuming that a law-making body will place provisions in legislation that are not intended to have a direct effect themselves.[8] If these sections have a greater purpose, then to what extent are they free-standing on their own or are they primarily there to provide context to other sections and help with their interpretation? The Court of Appeal has held, in the only case that has come before it, that the section was intended to be a free-standing provision and was enforceable on its own merits.[9] Whether this would be the case every time would probably depend on the wording of the section that was being considered and the context. The Welsh Government has sought to tackle the issue by making clear in its guidance on legislative drafting that overview sections should make very clear whether they are intended as mere summaries or to have direct effect in themselves.[10]

---

[8] See *Walker v Centaur Clothes Group* [2000] 2 All ER 589 @ 595

[9] *Jarvis v Evans* [2020] EWCA Civ 854.

[10] Writing laws for Wales: guidance on drafting legislation, para 2.4.
Available at https://gov.wales/writing-laws-for-wales-guidance-on-drafting-legislation.

CHAPTER THREE

RENTING HOMES:
AN OVERVIEW

The RHWA is intended to be a complete replacement for almost all existing residential tendencies, whether in the private or social sector. As such it replaces assured and assured shorthold tendencies under the Housing Act 1988, secure tendencies under the Housing Act 1985 and residential licences. It does not affect tenancies under the Rent Act 1977 or the Rent (Agriculture) Act 1976 but these are, of course, a dying breed.

The RHWA intended to create an entirely new, fully integrated, tenancy regime which brings together the private and social sectors making them partners in the provision of housing and eroding, at least from the tenant's perspective, the differences in the nature of their landlord.

Under the RHWA, all occupies of property all termed contract holders. This will be the case regardless of whether they are tenants or licensees. However, the common law status of tenants and licensees will be preserved. In fact, one of the key uncertainties created by the RHWA is how the common law status of tenants, but especially of licensees, will work alongside it. There are two types of contract available. The standard contract, which looks very like an assured shorthold tenancy, in that it only confers a right to occupy for a fixed period of time, and the secure contract which has most of the features of a secure tenancy. Regardless of the contract type, contract holders have a right to a written tenancy agreement and there are significant powers for the courts to step in and impose these if they are not provided. The written contracts are also subject to substantial interference from the worst government. All written contracts will have areas which they must compulsorily include. There will also be supplemental sections where there are elements of choice permitted but those choices will be tightly bounded. Finally, there will be sections where relative contractual freedom pertains provided that nothing undermines any of the sections set out but state.

The RHWA provides similar methods to recover possession as existing structures for rent arrears, breach of agreement and sale of property. However, it is more complex in structure as these provisions are spread across a number of different sections rather than being a series of defined grounds for possession Covered by one section of the RHWA. How this will work in practise in terms of statutory notices and the like remains to be seen. There are also powers equivalent to section 21 notices which allow recovery of possession at the end of a fixed term agreement without giving a specific reason. These of course only apply to standard contracts and not to secure contracts. Where a standard contract has been given by a social landlord they are also unable to avail themselves of this provision easily. However, the Welsh government has considered removing this provision altogether but instead is engaged in altering it so that, rather than being two months' notice not to expire sooner than six months, like a current section 21 notice, it is a much longer run regime. The new provisions will prevent notice being given at all within the first six months of the tenancy and a notice given will have a notice period of not less than six months. Effectively therefore, standard contract holders will have the certainty of a year in their property unless the landlord has a justification for recovering possession.

There has been a tremendously long delay between the passing of Renting Homes, back in 2016, and it being brought into effect. This has been for a number of reasons including difficulties in negotiating with the Ministry of Justice over court structures, lack of resources within the Welsh government, competing priorities, and varying degrees of political will at different times. However, things had started to progress in early 2020 with the Welsh Government stating that the RHWA would be in force before the Welsh Assembly elections in May of that year. The Covid-19 pandemic promptly put paid to that timeline but as we began to get on top of it a new implementation date in July 2022 was put forward. That date also slipped at relatively short notice with a final date of 1 December 2022 being set.

One of the unusual elements of the RHWA is the manner in which it comes into effect. From 1 December the RHWA will apply to all tenancies and licences within its scope and they will all automatically become occupation contracts on that day. This is in effect an "R day" with instant conversion. This has been unpopular, especially with larger landlords, because that will require all landlords to give their occupiers new contracts which comply with the Act in a relatively short period from that day. For larger landlords this is potentially a massive exercise. The RHWA provides a six-month implementation period for landlords to resolve the issue of agreements, but it seems almost inevitable that some landlords will fail to appreciate that the changes have occurred and will miss the deadline.

One of the issues created by the very long gestation period between passing of the RHWA and its implementation is that the terrain has moved, especially in the Private Rented Sector. England has advanced in terms of changes to electrical safety and Wales has had to slot provisions into the RHWA by way of regulations. Scotland has abandoned fixed term tenancies and evictions without cause altogether and Wales has sought to react to this by lengthening notice periods[11] before the RHWA came into force. It has also consulted on making these longer notice periods apply to existing private sector tenancies that have been converted into occupation contracts.[12] These changes have created an air of uncertainty around the introduction of the legislation as landlords perceive the ground shifting under their feet.

---

[11] In the Renting Homes (Amendment) (Wales) Act 2021.

[12] See https://gov.wales/written-statement-consultation-renting-homes-wales-act-2016-notice-periods-converted-contracts.

CHAPTER FOUR

WHO, WHAT AND WHERE?

Who does it apply to?

The RHWA applies to almost all rented properties in the private and social sector. It will affect any property rented on an Assured Shorthold Tenancy ("AST") and will also affect properties let on residential licences. It does not have high or low rent exceptions so will pick up tenancies that currently fall outside the Housing Act 1988. It will not affect old rentals which are subject to the Rent Act 1977 or lettings to companies. Likewise in the social sector all forms of secure tenancy and other supported tenancies offered by social landlords are covered by the RHWA.

The legislation affects tenancies immediately. So, all tenancies or licences that are within its scope will automatically convert on 1 December 2022 to become occupation contracts under the RHWA. Therefore, the law applying to them will change considerably on that date. There are transitional periods in place to allow a period for landlords to catch up with their obligations, but these are all strictly time limited.

Contracts

Under Renting Homes all tenancies and licences are called occupation contracts and occupiers are referred to as contract-holders. Landlords provide those occupation contracts to the contract-holders. The use of the phrase occupation contract is a little unfortunate. The Welsh government model contract makes things even more confusing by frequently shortening the phrase occupation contract to contract and then also using the word contract to describe the written agreement that it itself is. So, occupation contracts are a statutory construct but they involve a contractual relationship between the landlord and contract-holder. It is easy to get mixed up between the occupation contract as a legal creation of the RHWA and the contract as a common law agreement between the parties. In fact, in any RHWA-governed relationship both will exist.

Occupation contracts are split into two types:

1. standard contracts- provided mainly by private sector landlords offering limited security for a fixed period; and

2. secure contracts- provided mainly by community landlords offering substantial security on a relatively indefinite basis.

Standard contracts are also further split into periodic and fixed-term contracts.[13] Secure contracts are always periodic.[14]

A community landlord includes local authorities of varying types, registered social landlords, private registered providers of social housing, and housing co-operatives.[15] Private landlords are any landlord that does not fall into the category of a community landlord.[16] Private landlords are assumed to offer standard contracts while community landlords are assumed to offer secure contracts although there are some exceptions to these basic presumptions.[17]

---

[13] RHWA, s1.

[14] RHWA, s8(2).

[15] RHWA, s9.

[16] RHWA, s10.

[17] RHWA, s2(2).

Community landlords can offer standard contracts where specific exceptions apply.[18] These include:[19]

- Occupancy for nil rent;

- Occupancy for a holiday;

- Occupancy in a care institution;

- Occupancy on a temporary basis by someone who has entered as a trespasser;

- Occupancy in supported accommodation;

- Introductory occupation contracts;

- Accommodation provided for asylum seekers;

- Occupation provided for homeless persons;

- Service occupancies for police and fire service personnel and other specific types of employer where the employment contract requires the employee to occupy the premises as part of their duties;

- Student accommodation provided to enable the occupier to attend a prescribed course at a further or higher educational establishment;

---

[18] RHWA, s11.

[19] RHWA, Schedule 3.

- Occupancy where the land the dwelling is on has been acquired for development and the accommodation is provided on a temporary basis;

- Temporary occupancy for persons commencing employment where the employee has moved into the area;

- Occupancy in accommodation which was let by someone who is not a community landlord specifically for a community landlord to provide temporary housing;

- Temporary occupancy in a dwelling provided for temporary occupation while works are carried out on a dwelling previously occupied by the occupier as their home;

- Occupancy provided for key workers where the occupancy was not provided under allocation rules;

- Occupancy in a dwelling built by a social landlord with the intention of transferring it to a fully mutual housing association or a co-operative housing association.

Some of these require notice to be given before the occupancy commences[20] and there is a prescribed form for that notice.[21] Where such a notice is served a contract-holder in receipt of that notice has a right to apply to the county court for them to review the decision to make a contract a standard rather than a secure contract.[22] That application must be made inside the tight timeline of 14 days from service of the notice of the occupancy being a standard contract. The county court must treat the application as a form of judicial review and must apply the same

---

[20] RHWA, s13.

[21] Form RHW1.

[22] RHWA, s14.

criteria the High Court would in making a judicial review decision. The county court may confirm or quash the decision to serve the notice and may also make any other order the High Court might make on making a quashing order. If a notice is quashed the landlord has 14 days from the date of that order to serve a fresh notice.

Where a community landlord adopts a contract because they have offered a contract to someone else who has then (with consent) sub-contracts to another occupier or the contract-holder abandons their contract with the community landlord then if that sub-contract was a standard contract then it will continue as a standard contract with the community landlord. In any other case where a community landlord takes over a standard contract that standard contract will come to an end and a new secure contract with the community landlord will be created. This is subject to specific exceptions, mostly relating to scenarios where a community landlord would be able to offer a standard contract if they had granted it themselves in the first place.[23]

Other Community Landlord Contracts

Community landlords can also form three other types of contract.

The first of these is the introductory standard contract. A community landlord can form an introductory standard contract by giving the contract holder notice in advance that the contract will be a standard contract. The contract holder cannot have previously been a contract holder with that community landlord.[24] These contracts subsist as periodic standard contracts for the introductory period and they then end and are replaced with secure contracts automatically.[25] The introductory

---

[23] RHWA, s12.

[24] RHWA, schedule 3, para 3.

[25] RHWA, s16(1).

period is normally 12 months but it can be extended to 18 months[26] by the giving of notice not less than eight weeks before the end of the 12 month period.[27] The introductory period is also extended automatically if possession proceeding are commenced or notice has been given of intention to being possession proceedings in which case it runs until those proceedings end or the period during which proceedings can be taken on the notice expires.[28] If a notice is given to extend the introductory period it must give the reasons for that extension and must also advise the contract holder that they can seek a review of that decision[29] and that they have 14 days to make such a review request.[30] Reviews are initially made to the landlord but can then be made to the county court if the review is refused.[31] The manner of such a review can be,[32] and is, prescribed by regulations.[33]

The second type of contract is the supported standard contract.[34] A supported standard contract is a contract where the landlord is a community landlord or a registered charity and they are providing accommodation and also providing, or arranging for someone to provide on their behalf, support services which are connected with that accommodation. This does not include care institutions, but the RHWA specifically mentions addiction support, help in finding employment or permanent accommodation, and support for those who have difficulty with independent living. So it is clear that the intent of the RHWA is to

---

[26] RHWA, schedule 4, para 1(1).

[27] RHWA, schedule 4, para 3.

[28] RHWA, schedule 4, para 1(2).

[29] RHWA, Schedule 4, para 3(3) and 3(4).

[30] RHWA, Schedule 4, para 4(2).

[31] RHWA, Schedule 4, para 5.

[32] RHWA, s203.

[33] The Renting Homes (Review of Decisions) (Wales) Regulations 2022.

[34] RHWA, s143.

focus on accommodation with tightly linked support intended to accomplish a wider social aim. Supported standard contracts, as well as being standard rather than secure contracts have other provisions associated with them. First, supported standard contracts can have what the RHWA refers to as mobility.[35] In other words they do not have to attach to any specific property and can contain a provision that they apply to any dwelling that the landlord notifies the tenant that the contract applies to. This is an interesting position which has implications for the common law estate offered. It is generally accepted that a tenancy must be for identified land and where the landlord has a right to move an occupier at their discretion then such a power negates the existence of exclusive possession and makes the occupation a licence rather than a tenancy.[36] Therefore, to the extent that it is relevant a supported standard contract which includes a mobility provision would create a licence rather than a tenancy. However, a supported standard contract without a mobility provision would likely lead to a creation of a tenancy. It was precisely this distinction that the RHWA was intended to render irrelevant but there are likely to be scenarios, albeit rare, where the distinction continues to matter. Supported standard contracts also allow for the exclusion of contract holders in specific circumstances. More on this later.

Finally, community landlords can form a prohibited conduct standard contract although they cannot do this by themselves and it is in fact something the courts will impose. Community or charity landlords under secure contracts may apply to the court to have an order made on the basis that a contract-holder has committed anti-social behaviour or some other conduct prohibited by the RHWA. The court may make an order if they are satisfied that the conduct has occurred and that they would, if it had been sought, have made a possession order. The court must also be satisfied that the landlord will provide support to the contract-holder to help them correct their behaviour and that the order is reasonable. If

---

[35] RHWA, s144.

[36] *Dresden Estate v Collinson* [1987] 1 WLUK 1054.

such an order is made the secure contract converts to a periodic standard contract.[37] This happens for the probation period and at the end of the probation period the contract automatically converts back to a secure contract.[38] Before applying to court the landlord must notify the contract-holder of their intention to apply to court for an order, although the court can dispense with that requirement if it considers it reasonable. The notice must specify the date before which a court application will not be made and a date after which it will not be made. The first date can be the same day that the notice is served while the last date can be any date up to a maximum of six months from the date of service of the notice.[39] The notice must be made on the appropriate prescribed form.[40] If an order is made the probation period is ordinarily for 12 months. The landlord can serve notice shortening the probation period[41] using the appropriate prescribed form.[42] A contract-holder may also apply to the county court to request them to terminate the probation period early at any point after they have been through six months of probation.[43] The landlord can also serve notice extending the probation period up to a maximum of 18 months,[44] again using the appropriate prescribed form.[45] If an extension is sought the contract-holder may request the landlord to review the decision within 14 days.[46] If the landlord on review confirms the notice then the contract holder may apply to the county court for a review of that decision. The county court review proceeds in much the

---

[37] RHWA, s116.

[38] RHWA, s117.

[39] RHWA, Schedule 7, para 1.

[40] Form RHW35.

[41] RHWA, Schedule 7, para 3.

[42] Form RHWA36.

[43] RHWA, Schedule 7, para 7.

[44] RHWA, Schedule 7, para 4.

[45] Form RHWA37.

[46] RHWA, Schedule 7, para 5.

same manner as the review that can be sought of a decision by a community landlord to impose a standard contract.[47]

Other Exceptions

There are further exceptions to the formation of an occupation contract at all. First, an occupation only falls within the RHWA if it is made with an individual and "confers on the individual the right to occupy a dwelling as a home". Therefore any contract made with a corporate entity or which is for a property that is not intended as a dwelling (a holiday home for example) will fall outside the terms of the RHWA.[48] The legislation also requires that "rent or other consideration" is payable for the accommodation.[49] So, if no consideration is payable then no occupation contract exists. However, there is no maximum or minimum rent figures as found in the Housing Act 1988 so high value tenancies will fall within the RHWA.

A further detailed set of exceptions is also found in the RHWA.[50] A number of occupancies will not fall within the RHWA unless notice is given that they should do so. These include:

- Where the occupancy is for the benefit of someone other than a person named in the occupancy agreement;

- Which is for holiday accommodation;

- Which relates to the provision of accommodation in a hospital, care home, or children's home;

---

[47] RHWA, Schedule 7, para 6.

[48] RHWA, s7(2).

[49] RHWA, s7(1).

[50] RHWA, Schedule 2.

- Which is a temporary expedient where the person it is made with entered the property as a trespasser;

- Where the accommodation is shared with the landlord.[51]

Other occupations can never fall within the RHWA. These include where:

- All of the occupiers are under 18;

- The occupancy is a tenancy governed by Part 2 of the Landlord and Tenant Act 1954;

- The occupancy is a statutory tenancy under the Rent (Agriculture) Act 1976 or a protected tenancy or statutory tenancy under the Rent Act 1977;

- The occupancy is a tenancy of an agricultural holding of a farm business tenancy under the Agricultural Holdings Act 1986 or the Agricultural Tenancies Act 1995;

- The occupancy is a tenancy of over 21 years;

- The occupancy relates to armed forces accommodation or is provided by a charity or community landlord for no more than 24 hours at a time.[52]

---

[51] RHWA, Schedule 2, Parts 1 & 2.

[52] RHWA, Schedule 2, Part 3.

Standard Contracts

Where a contract is not made with a community landlord as defined in the RHWA then it is assumed to be made with a private landlord.[53] Private landlords generally form standard contracts, although with a couple of exceptions.[54] Private landlords can elect to form secure contracts by giving notice that the contract will be a secure contract before it is formed. Interestingly, there is no prescribed form for this notice, which is a little unusual as forms have been prescribed for almost every eventuality by the Welsh government! Private landlords are also not permitted to make a standard contract where the occupier was already a contract holder under a secure contract.

Fixed Term and Periodic Contracts

It is possible to form both fixed term and periodic contracts. Secure contracts are all periodic. Although community landlords can make fixed term contracts these are not secure contracts. Standard contracts can be fixed term or periodic. In keeping with the evolution of standard contracts from Assured Shorthold Tenancies, where a fixed term standard contract comes to an end then a new periodic standard contract is automatically formed on similar terms and conditions arising from the end of the fixed term.

Contract structure

The RHWA relies heavily on the occupation contract to enforce much of its regulation. It operates rather like the statutory repairing obligations found in residential tenancies in England (and prior to the RHWA in

---

[53] RHWA, s10.

[54] RHWA, s17.

Wales as well).[55] That is by requiring specific terms to be inserted into occupation-contracts and implying their existence if they are not inserted.

The RHWA splits the various terms it requires into:

- Fundamental;

- Supplementary; and

- Additional;

provisions. When these provisions are actually inserted into a contract they are called fundamental, supplementary and additional terms. In this text I will call these all terms as the provision/term distinction is somewhat artificial.

Fundamental terms are those terms specified by the RHWA itself. Some of them must be incorporated into an occupation contract entirely unchanged. Some of them can be modified but only by agreement between the landlord and the contract-holder and only if they "improve the contract-holder's position".[56] However, it is unclear whether the required level of agreement is fulfilled by simply having both parties sign a modified occupation contract or whether something more is needed. Given that the RHWA requires that omitted fundamental provisions are identified then it seems likely that the signing of an occupation contract is enough. The legislation states that terms must be identified as not incorporated but this provision also refers to situations where terms have been modified so the presumption must be that modifications must also be identified.[57]

---

[55] Provided by s11, Landlord and Tenant Act 1985.

[56] RHWA, s3(3).

[57] RHWA, s32(3)(a).

Supplementary terms are those further terms that are required to be inserted by regulations.[58] As with fundamental terms they can be omitted or modified by agreement but there is no further limitation that the omission or modification must improve the contract-holder's position.[59] However, as with fundamental terms that omission must be made clear.[60]

Additional terms are those other terms that a landlord and contract-holder might agree between themselves. The only restriction on these is that they cannot be structured so as to undermine or override a fundamental or supplementary term and if they do they will be ineffective.[61]

Finally, contracts must also contain key matters. These are not terms and will be different for every contract. They are the key pieces of information without which the contract just would not work. This includes such things as:

- the address of the dwelling;

- the occupation date;

- the amount of rent or other consideration;

- the rental periods;

- whether the contract is periodic or made for a fixed term;

- if it is for a fixed term, what that fixed term is;

---

[58] RHWA, s23(1). Currently set out in the Renting Homes (Supplementary Provisions) (Wales) Regulations 2022.

[59] RHWA, s24.

[60] RHWA, s32(3)(b).

[61] RHWA, s28.

- any periods during which the contract-holder is not entitled to occupy the dwelling as a home.[62]

Model Contracts

Welsh Ministers are obliged to provide model occupation contracts. They do not have to provide them for all occupation contract types or all scenarios but the wording of the RHWA suggests that they must provide something.[63] In fact, the Welsh Ministers have provided model agreements for all contract types.[64] A model agreement must incorporate, unmodified, all the fundamental and supplementary terms applicable to that contract type.[65] It is open to doubt how successful the model agreements are. This is potentially a serious problem for the legislation in practical use as the model contracts are likely to be used for a lot of occupation contracts and will come to characterise how it is perceived. However, the model agreements are long and wordy. They do not really meet the aspirations of the RHWA as they frequently refer to sections of the Act when describing rights and obligations and so they are not in fact the self-contained documents that was suggested when the Act was being passed. In practice many landlords and contract-holders are likely to find the model contracts confusing and hard to use. Given that there are typographical errors in the model contracts there will also be the concern that they contain a mistake of some description which might render them not in compliance with the RHWA.

There is also the danger that landlords will see the model contracts as the be all and end all of what they need to provide, not appreciating the

---

[62] RHWA, ss26 & 27.

[63] RHWA, s29(1).

[64] In the Renting Homes (Model Written Statements of Contract) (Wales) Regulations 2022.

[65] RHWA, s29(2).

requirement to give prescribed forms setting out the landlord's address, for example.

Converted Contracts

As from 1 December 2022 the RHWA immediately applies to any tenancy or licence that falls within its remit, including those already in existence. However, it would be unreasonable to expect immediate compliance with all the provisions of the RHWA instantly. Therefore for converted contracts there is a period of time to comply.

A converted contract is one which existed immediately before 1 December 2022.[66] Such contracts will continue to be converted contracts both for themselves and for any further periodic or fixed term occupation contract which arises from it. Those converted contracts are deemed to be occupation contracts which commence as from 1 December 2022.[67]

The RHWA specifies in some detail what type of occupation contract each existing tenancy or licence is to become. There are various exceptions based on more unusual scenarios but the table below sets out in general terms what type of occupation contract pre-RHWA tenancies and licences will become.

---

[66] RHWA, Schedule 12, para 1.

[67] RHWA, s240.

Pre RHWA Tenancy or Licence Type	RHWA Contract Type
Introductory tenancy	Introductory standard contract
Assured Shorthold Tenancy granted by a social landlord or a private registered provider of social housing which was described as a "starter tenancy"	Introductory standard contract
Demoted tenancies	Prohibited conduct standard contract
Assured shorthold tenancy or licence relating to supported accommodation	Supported standard contract
Assured shorthold tenancy, assured tenancy, assured agricultural occupancy made by a private landlord	Fixed term or periodic standard contract as appropriate
Secure contract made by a private or community landlord	Secure contract

Trespassers

There is another category of persons who can have a contract made for them through the RHWA, that is those who are trespassing on property. Traditionally, it was fairly difficult for a trespasser to acquire a right as a tenant or a licensee and they really had to look to the longer-term and hope to acquire title by way of adverse possession. The RHWA changes this. If a person trespasses in a property that is not already subject to an occupation contract and makes payments to the person who would normally be entitled to evict them for that occupation then they may be able to acquire a contract to occupy the property. Note that there is no requirement that those payments be of any appropriate value but simply that they must be made and accepted with the person accepting them either aware that the person they are being made by is trespasser or they should be aware that that person is a trespasser. If those payments are accepted and the trespasser remains in the property for more than two months from the date of the first payment without possession proceedings being commenced against them then they will be deemed to have been granted a periodic occupation contract. Demonstrating the agnosticism of the RHWA in respect of tenancies and licences there is a specific statement that the occupation contract is "either a tenancy or a licence" and in fact neither are implied by these provisions. The reality of the RHWA is of course that whether the contract is a tenancy or licence (or neither) does not much matter for most practical purposes. The nature of the occupation contract is not specified so it will be either standard or secure depending on the nature of the landlord concerned. The terms of the occupation contract are those provided for by the RHWA and the rent sum and rental periods are based on those paid by the trespasser. Therefore if a trespasser was able to find a property controlled by a community landlord, obtain access to it, and make payments in respect of it for two months they would be have a good possibility of being able to assert they were a secure contract-holder under the RHWA.[68]

---

[68] RHWA, s238.

CHAPTER FIVE

INFORMATION

Written Statements

All contract holders in Wales are entitled under the RHWA to a written statement of their contract. This information is relatively detailed and long-winded. The RHWA specifically requires that many of the provisions in the Act are set out in the contract with the occupier. This is partly due to a desire to give occupiers and landlords a single document which has all of their rights and obligations in it. It is also appears to be due to a degree of uncertainty as to the powers of the Welsh government and so the placing of all the obligations in an occupation contract avoids a scenario where the courts find that the Welsh government does not have the power to impose an obligation directly in law.

The requirement is to provide the written statement within 14 days of the date the property is occupied. This would seem to suggest that any provision of the written statement prior to occupation will not be in compliance with the requirements of the RHWA. This seems a severe consequence which it is hard to imagine could have been intended. If the narrowest possible reading is adopted then that would suggest that a landlord who signs an occupation contract with an occupier and gives them the relevant information along with the keys to the property would be in breach of the legislative requirement because it would have been given prior to the occupation date rather than within 14 days beginning with the occupation date.[69] A more sensible reading is that the written statement must be given to the contract-holder on a long-stop basis such that it is given within 14 days of occupation. However, giving it before occupation is permissible. If this question were to come before the

---

[69] RHWA, s31(1).

appellate courts that second, looser reading, is likely to be the one they choose to adopt.

Contracts that arise by conversion must also get these new contracts within 6 months of the 1 December conversion date.[70] After that point the landlord will be in breach of the obligation to provide a written agreement and subject to penalties.

A written agreement must include all the prescribed:[71]

- key matters;

- fundamental terms and where they have been (legitimately) modified or omitted those modifications must be identified;

- supplementary terms and where these have been omitted then that omission must be identified; and

- additional terms if required.

In practice this means that most RHWA written agreements are likely to have areas of strike through where omissions and modifications have been made.

It is a fundamental provision of an RHWA occupation agreement that a written statement is given. This is somewhat circular in that the requirement to provide a written statement must be written into the very written statement that the RHWA and the written statement itself requires. If that clause is omitted then it hardly be enforced under the terms of the written statement and the RHWA will need to step in.[72]

---

[70] RHWA, Schedule 12, para 11.

[71] RHWA, s32.

[72] RHWA, s31(7).

Explanatory Information

There is a further requirement to have a written explanation of the agreement and what it is. This further information forms a part of the written statement. The things that must be included are set out in regulations but the exact wording is not prescribed.[73] The regulations state that the explanatory information must set out:

- That the document is a written statement of an occupation contract;

- That the occupation contract is made under the RHWA;

- The meanings under the RHWA of:

  - "occupation date";

  - "key matters";

- An explanation of the key elements of:

  - fundamental terms;

  - supplementary terms;

  - additional terms;

- How unincorporated fundamental or supplementary are identified within the written statement;

- The statutory time periods for the giving of the written statement to the contract-holder;

---

[73] See the Renting Homes (Explanatory Information for Written Statements of Occupation Contracts) (Wales) Regulations 2022

- The penalties for failing to provide the written statement on time;

- That the written statement can be provided electronically if that is agreed;

- That the written statement sets out the rights and responsibilities of the contract-holder and the landlord;

- That the contract-holder should read the terms of the written statement to ensure they fully understand them and they agree they reflect the modifications to terms or additional terms agreed between the contract-holder and landlord;

- That the contract-holder should keep the written statement of the occupation contract safe as they may need to refer to it in the future;

- Sign-posting for more information to the Welsh Government website, to advice agencies and legal advisors;

- Disputes over the terms of an occupation contract may be determined in the county court;

- That contract-holders who have an issue with their dwelling should first contact their landlord to try and resolve the issue but they can then contact advice agencies or independent legal advisors who may be able to assist;

- Any additional term, or modification to a supplementary term, that is incorporated in the occupation contract is not binding on the contract-holder if it is an unfair term;

- That the contract-holder cannot be evicted without a court order, unless they abandon the dwelling;

- That the contract-holder has important rights on their use of the dwelling although some of these are require obtaining the landlord's consent;

- That the contract-holder will be liable for any anti-social behaviour or other prohibited conduct of anyone who lives in or visits the dwelling and the things that might constitute anti-social behaviour or prohibited conduct;

- That a succession right may apply to someone who lives in the dwelling with the contract-holder;

- That the contract-holder must not allow the dwelling to become overcrowded and the statutory basis for determining this[74] and that overcrowding may constitute prohibited conduct.

- That before any possession order can be made the landlord must demonstrate that all the correct procedures have been followed and that one of the statutory bases for possession is made out and none of the statutory defences apply.

Depending on the type of occupation contract there are further elements to the explanatory information that must be given.

So, for a standard contract which is periodic from the start the explanatory information must also specify that the contract-holder's contract is periodic and continues from one rental period to the next.

For an introductory standard contract and prohibited conduct standard contract the explanatory information must also make clear that unless the occupation contract is extended or otherwise terminated, at the end of

---

[74] Part 10, Housing Act 1985.

the period for which it is made, the contract will become a secure contract.

In a supported standard contract the explanatory information must set out the powers to temporarily exclude a contract holder from the dwelling.

Finally, in a secure contract the explanatory information must set out the bases by which possession can be sought by the landlord and that the secure contract is periodic and continues from one rental period to the next.

In practice it is likely that many landlords will use the wording from the Welsh Government's model agreement. However, this contains mistakes. For example, the wording in the model agreement states that the landlord must identify modifications made to supplementary terms. In fact, this is incorrect and landlords must only identify omissions made to supplementary terms. They are not required to identify modifications of supplementary terms. This may in fact be an error in the original RHWA and it may well have been the intent of drafters that modifications would have to be identified.

Landlord Information

As well as the explanatory information and statement of the terms of the occupation contract a landlord must also provide a contract holder within the same time period with "notice of an address to which the contract-holder may send documents that are intended for the landlord".[75] If that address changes then the contract holder must be given the new address within 14 days.[76] If the landlord changes then the new landlord must, within 14 days of becoming the landlord, give the

---

[75] RHWA, s39(1).

[76] RHWA, s39(2)

same information.[77] This requirement is a more formal statement of the existing legislative requirement that is being replaced by the RHWA.[78] Although, unlike the existing legislation which requires an address to be given that is within the jurisdiction of England and Wales there is no similar obligation here and therefore such an address could in principle be anywhere. Forms are prescribed for all of these scenarios. While those forms are not precisely compulsory in that the relevant forms regulations specify that a "notice or other document in a form substantially to the same effect as the prescribed form is valid"[79] it would be risky to use an alternative document. This creates something of a trap for the unwary in that many landlords are likely to assume that by having their address in the occupation agreement then it has been notified to the contract holder while a strict reading of the RHWA and the regulations would suggest that this is insufficient.

Time Limits and Enforcement

A written statement and the other associated information must be provided without any charge "before the end of the period of 14 days starting with the occupation date".[80] This may create something of a potential trap. Written statements are commonly provided before occupation, at the time the contract is signed between landlord (or agent) and contract-holder. If the contract holder is to occupy later than the signing of the occupation contract then it may be that the written statement cannot be given until they move in. Alternatively, the wording may be intended to mean that the written statement can be given at any

---

[77] RHWA, s39(2).

[78] Section 48, Landlord and Tenant Act 1987.

[79] Regulation 3(2), Renting Homes (Prescribed Forms) (Wales) Regulations 2022.

[80] RHWA, s31(1).

stage but must be given at the latest within 14 days after the contract holder moves in.

If the identity of the contract-holder changes then a new written statement must be provided within 14 days of that change.[81] Until the written statement is provided or the new contract holder occupies the property then the terms of the occupation contract are not enforceable on them.[82]

Contract holders may also request further written statements at any time and must be provided with them within 14 days of request but they can be charged a reasonable fee for their provision.[83] If a fee is being charged for the further statement then the 14 day window to provide the further statement does not start until the fee has been paid.[84]

Where a landlord fails to provide a written statement at all or it is incomplete then a contract holder can apply to the court to have the court provide a written statement[85] or to complete an incomplete statement.[86] If the incomplete statement is missing fundamental or supplementary terms then those terms must be incorporated by the court without modification unless it is asserted by the contract holder that that term was not incorporated or was modified. Therefore, the contract holder at that point has substantial control over the terms of the tenancy.

In both cases the court may also decide to award compensation calculated on the basis of the rent due for each day the breach persists up to a

---

81 RHWA, s31(2).

82 RHWA, s42(2).

83 RHWA, s31.

84 RHWA, s31(6)(b).

85 RHWA, s34.

86 RHWA, s36.

maximum of two months.[87] Interest then also falls to be paid on the compensation calculated on a per day basis at the statutory rate[88] from the end of two months after the start of the tenancy for missing statements or on such basis as the court thinks fit for incomplete statements. Where compensation is due to the contract holder they may set that off against rent, and by extension against arrears of rent.[89]

As a further potential incentive, a contract holder is free to walk away from the contract and no term of an occupation contract can be enforced on them up until they either move in or a written statement is given.[90] This does not sit well with the requirement to give the written statement within 14 days of occupation. If the interpretation I have laid out above is right and a written statement cannot be given until after the occupation date then a contract holder cannot have a term of an occupation contract enforced until they move in and the provision is largely nugatory. None of this sits well with the provisions of the fee legislation which permits holding deposits to be charged for the "grant of a standard occupation contract".[91] If this is all correct then a contract holder can pay the holding deposit, sign the occupation contract and have the holding deposit credited to their rent or returned to them, and then say they do not want to move in, presumably then recovering their money. This makes a nonsense of the entire process.

In truth it would seem likely that a higher court would elect to read the legislation as meaning that once a written statement is given a contract holder is bound to the contract they have made.[92] There is also the side

---

[87] RHWA, s87.

[88] As provided for in s6, Late Payment of Commercial Debts (Interest) Act 1998

[89] RHWA, s88.

[90] RHWA, s42(1).

[91] Schedule 1, Para 4, Renting Homes (Fees etc.) (Wales) Act 2019.

[92] RHWA, s31(1).

point that even if the RHWA allows a contract-holder to walk away there is a contract between the parties and it may be that the terms of that are enforceable independently of the RHWA.

Further contracts

Where a fixed term standard contract comes to an end then a new periodic contract will be formed arising from the end of the existing fixed term contract.[93] Interestingly those contracts are not formed on exactly the same terms and conditions. The RHWA states that the periodic contract will have the same rental periods as the original fixed term.[94] This would seem to be a problem if a landlord seeks rent in advance. If the contract-holder is asked to pay six month's rent in advance in a fixed term then a periodic contract arising from that fixed term would have the same six monthly rental period. This is an issue that has arisen before.[95] The new periodic contract will also incorporate all fundamental and supplementary terms without modification.[96] The meaning of this is a little uncertain. It may simply mean that the original terms from the fixed term contract are carried over to the periodic contract unmodified. However, it may also mean that fundamental and supplementary terms in the periodic contract are reset to the statutory wording of them. This means that if a fixed term contract has modifications to fundamental and supplementary terms then those will disappear as it ends and a periodic contract succeeds to it unless a new periodic contract is created which re-incorporates those modifications or the original fixed term contract includes a provision to specify that the ensuring periodic contract will contain the same modifications to fundamental and supplementary terms as the original. This would seem to be the more likely reading as it is in keeping with the use of modified terms in the RHWA more generally

---

[93] RHWA, s184(3)(a).

[94] RHWA, s184(3)(b).

[95] *Church Commissioners for England v Meya* [2006] EWCA Civ 821.

[96] RHWA, s184(4).

and there is also a specific legislative provision allowing for the clarification of terms to be carried over into a periodic tenancy from a fixed term.[97]

Converted Contracts

Where a tenancy or licence exists before the coming into force of the RHWA on 1 December 2022 then the RHWA will immediately apply to it. However, there is a period of time to provide the necessary written statements and other information. This is six months from the commencement of the RHWA, that is by 1 June 2023. As long as written statements are provided by that date the requirements of the RHWA have been met and application to court by contract-holders and other penalties are in abeyance until that time. After 1 June 2023, however, any landlord who has not complied with the information requirements of the RHWA is in default of the legislation.[98]

---

[97] RHWA, s185.

[98] RHWA, Schedule 12, paras 11-13.

CHAPTER SIX

DEPOSITS

There has long been regulation of security deposits paid by private-sector tenants in both England and Wales.[99] The RHWA largely re-enacts that legislation in much the same wording and makes little change to the existing regime other than extending it to cover all forms of contract covered by the RHWA. Therefore, it is likely that much of the existing case law relating to tenancy deposits will continue to be applicable to the RHWA deposit regime.

So, just as is the case now, there are three key obligations in relation to tenancy deposits under the RHWA: [100]

1. To protect the deposit with an approved scheme;

2. To comply with the initial requirements of an approve scheme within 30 days of deposit receipt;

3. To give the contract-holder along with anyone who has paid the deposit on their behalf the information prescribed in regulations within 30 days of deposit receipt.

The RHWA defines the initial requirements of a prescribed scheme as being "the requirements of the scheme which must be complied with by the landlord when a deposit is paid".[101] This largely replicates the wording of the existing structure.[102] It is generally felt that the initial requirements are little more than those basic procedural requirements

---

[99] Under Chapter 4, Part 6, Housing Act 2004.

[100] RHWA, s46.

[101] RHWA s47(1).

[102] S213(4), Housing Act 2004.

imposed by schemes in order to have the deposit registered with them. They certainly cannot be used to gold-plate the legislation.[103]

There are regulations under the RHWA which set out the prescribed information[104] just as was the case in pre-cursor systems.[105] In fact the regulations are almost exactly the same as the existing ones with the terminology amended to reflect the differences created by the RHWA. So the contract holder must be given:

1. the name, address, telephone number and email address of deposit scheme administrator;

2. information from the scheme administrator explaining how the deposit provisions under the RHWA work;

3. the procedures that apply under the scheme by to enable sums from the deposit to be repair to the contract-holder at the end of the occupation contract;

4. the procedures that apply under the scheme where either landlord or contract-holder are not contactable at the end of the occupation contract;

5. the procedures that apply under the scheme where the landlord and the contract-holder dispute the amount to repaid to the contract-holder at the end of the occupation contract;

6. the scheme facilities to enable deposit to be resolved without litigation;

---

[103] *Draycott & Anor v Hannells Letting Ltd (t/a Hannells Letting Agents)* [2010] EWHC 217.

[104] The Renting Homes (Deposit Schemes) (Required Information) (Wales) Regulations 2022.

[105] The Housing (Tenancy Deposits) (Prescribed Information) Order 2007.

7. the amount of the deposit paid;

8. the address of the dwelling to which the occupation contract relates;

9. the name, address, telephone number and any e-mail address of the landlord;

10. the name, address, telephone number and any e-mail address of the contract-holder, including details that should be used by the landlord or scheme administrator for the purpose of contacting them at the end of the occupation contract;

11. the name, address, telephone number and any e-mail address of any person who paid the deposit on behalf of the contract-holder;

12. the circumstances when all or part of the deposit may be retained by the landlord, by reference to the terms of the occupation contract; and

13. confirmation (in the form of a certificate signed by the landlord) that the information in points 7 to 12 inclusive is accurate to the best of the landlord's knowledge and belief.

The contract holder must be given a similar opportunity to sign the prescribed information document to confirm its accuracy as well.

Interestingly the wording of the RHWA does not state, as the existing legislation does, that "references to a landlord or landlords in relation to any shorthold tenancy or tenancies include references to a person or persons acting on his or their behalf".[106] Therefore, it appears that letting agents do not have liability under the RHWA for failures of the deposit

---

[106] See s212(9)(a), Housing Act 2004.

legislation as they assuredly do under the existing regime.[107] At first blush it might also appear that letting agents also cannot sign the prescribed information certificate for a landlord. However, the existing case law states that a person authorised by the landlord to sign who signs for them is completing the required information "substantially to the like effect" as that required by the regulations and was therefore valid. The same position is likely to apply to situations where an authorised employee signs on behalf of a landlord that is incorporated in whatever manner.[108]

Again, as with the existing structure there are penalties for not complying with the statutory obligations. A contract-holder or any person who paid the deposit on their behalf may apply to the county court on the basis that either the initial requirements of a scheme have not been complied with (in practice this means that the deposit has not been registered)[109] or that they have not received the prescribed information[110] within 30 days of payment of the deposit. There is however a third possible basis for a claim to be made. This is that the contract-holder or person paying the deposit on their behalf has been informed that a deposit is being held by a specific scheme but is not able to obtain confirmation from that scheme administrator that the deposit is with the scheme.[111] This in fact closes a loophole with the existing regime in that it was theoretically lawful for a landlord to register a deposit with a scheme and then to move it to different scheme or even de-register it without informing the tenant that this had happened and with the tenant unable to do much about it. However, it also creates a new point for landlords under the RHWA to

---

[107] *Draycott & Anor v Hannells Letting Ltd (t/a Hannells Letting Agents)* [2010] EWHC 217.

[108] *Northwood (Solihull) Ltd v Fearn & Ors* [2022] EWCA Civ 40.

[109] RHWA, Schedule 5, para 2(2).

[110] RHWA, Schedule 5, para 2(3).

[111] RHWA, Schedule 5, para 2(4).

be wary of in that they must ensure that the deposit is registered with the scheme that the contract-holder has been told it is with.

If the court finds that one of the three bases for a claim are made out then it must order the person who holds the deposit to either return it in full to the person making the claim or to pay it into a custodial scheme.[112] In addition the court must order a further financial penalty of between one and three times the sum of the deposit to be paid to the claimant by the landlord.[113]

There are similar provisions within the RHWA for scenarios where the occupation contract has ended but where there are breaches of the deposit legislation. The main difference is that there is no scope for the court to order that the deposit is paid into a scheme.[114]

Again, as with the existing legislation there are provisions which make it unlawful for any deposit to be taken that is not paid as money so it is not lawful to accept valuable objects in lieu of a deposit. However, there is no problem with accepting a guarantee and the RHWA is specific that this is permitted.[115] The legislation is silent on the issue of deposit replacement schemes. These are not specifically prohibited but these schemes are clearly not money and they are not precisely a guarantee either. The fees legislation does not prohibit them and they are growing in popularity and so it is inevitable that the courts will find themselves having to resolve this issue.

Just as with the existing legislation, there have also been provisions inserted into the RHWA[116] which restrict the termination of a standard

---

[112] RHWA, Schedule 5, para 2(6).

[113] RHWA, Schedule 5, para 2(7).

[114] RHWA, Schedule 5, para 3.

[115] RHWA, s43.

[116] By the Renting Homes (Wales) Act 2016 (Amendment of Schedule 9A) Regulations 2022.

contract for the various termination provisions that exist in those contracts where a specific cause does not need to be shown. Where a deposit has not been dealt with correctly then these notices cannot be served.[117] At any point where a scheme's initial requirements have not been complied with, the prescribed information has not been given, or the deposit is not being held within an approved scheme then notice cannot be given unless the deposit has been returned or deductions agreed with the contract holder or a claim for breaches of the deposit legislation has been commenced and withdrawn, dealt with by the court, or resolved by agreement. It seems that the legislation was probably intended to mean that in all these scenarios no fix was available other than returning the deposit or court proceedings. However, the way the paragraph is worded suggests that a partial fix is possible by simply protecting the deposit late. This would not provide protection against the various financial penalties but would allow service of a notice. It is open to doubt whether the initial requirements of a scheme can be complied with at some later stage as the use of the word "initial" does suggest that they must be complied with at the outset. Depending on the manner of interpretation of this paragraph the RHWA deposit provisions could be either more or less restrictive on late protection than the existing regime.

Converted Contracts

For any contract that is converted under the RHWA the deposit legislation does not apply save for one specific group. These are converted contracts that were Assured Shorthold Tenancies immediately prior to conversion.[118] Further, for all these contracts the pre-existing deposit protection and service of notices is valid. Therefore, at least initially, there are relatively few deposits that will need dealing with specifically under the RHWA although this will grow quickly. The largest issue is likely to be the application to further types of tenancy and residential licence and

---

[117] RHWA, Schedule 9A, para 4.

[118] RHWA, Schedule 12, para 13A.

the steep learning curve for landlords that have never had to deal with deposits before.

CHAPTER SEVEN

REPAIRS

The RHWA has tried to create wholly new system for repairs. The original proposals have however ended up being somewhat watered down in practice and are only a limited advance on what was there already. In addition, as the world has moved on quite quickly in housing terms since the RHWA was passed in 2016, what was then seen as a substantial forward push in property standards and enforcement looks rather less impressive when compared with the steps taken by other UK jurisdictions between 2016 and today. This has also meant that substantial new obligations have been added in regulations shortly before the RHWA has come into effect.

The repairing obligations imposed by the RHWA fall into three areas:

1. An obligation to put and keep a property fit for human habitation;

2. An obligation to repair; and

3. A series of further certifications and specific safety equipment to be supplied.

Fitness for Human Habitation

The RHWA requires that any property let on a standard or secure contract is put and kept in a position that is fit for human habitation. There is an exemption for fixed terms in excess of seven years.[119] There are specific provisions on determining whether a fixed term tenancy is for

---

[119] RHWA, s91.

more or less than seven years.[120] These are very similar to existing similar provisions in statutory repairing obligations.[121] So any period before the occupation contract commences is discounted, as is any lease for more than seven years which contains a break clause for the landlord at less than seven years. However a lease of less than seven years with an option to renew for the contract-holder which will take it to over seven years is counted as a lease for more than seven years.

When considering fitness for human habitation, further matters can, and have been, prescribed by the Welsh Ministers.[122] These are not things which in and of themselves determine fitness but they are things that must be considered when deciding whether a property is or is not fit for human habitation. The broad areas are:

1.	Damp, mites and mould or fungal growth
2.	Cold
3.	Heat
4.	Asbestos and manufactured mineral fibres
5.	Biocides
6.	Carbon monoxide and fuel combustion products
7.	Lead
8.	Radiation
9.	Uncombusted fuel gas

---

[120] RHWA, s90.

[121] See s13(2), Landlord and Tenant Act 1985.

[122] In the Schedule to the Renting Homes (Fitness for Human Habitation) (Wales) Regulations 2022.

10.	Volatile organic compounds
11.	Crowding and space
12.	Entry by intruders
13.	Lighting
14.	Noise
15.	Domestic hygiene, pests and refuse
16.	Food safety
17.	Personal hygiene, sanitation and drainage
18.	Water supply
19.	Falls associated with baths etc.
20.	Falling on surfaces
21.	Falling on stairs etc.
22.	Falling between surfaces
23.	Electrical hazards
24.	Fire
25.	Flames, hot surfaces etc.
26.	Collision and entrapment
27.	Explosions
28.	Position and operability of amenities etc
29.	Structural collapse and falling elements

These areas are essentially the same as the Housing Health and Safety Rating System (HHSRS) assessment categories.[123] Originally, consideration was given to mandating that no category 1 HHSRS hazards should exist in a property, as is found in the Decent Homes Standard.[124] However, that was not what occurred and while the same criteria have been used to define fitness under the RHWA the HHSRS is not a definitional mechanism for this purpose. Undoubtedly though the HHSRS and its guidance will end up being a key means of deciding whether or not a property is fit. While a very similar system been operating in England for some time,[125] there is no substantial consideration by the senior courts which is of value but the similarity between England and Wales in their use of the HHSRS criteria means that decisions of the courts in relation to one are likely to be of value in understanding the other.

There is a reasonable expense exemption to the requirement to put and keep a property fit for human habitation. There is also an exemption for unfitness caused by fire, storm, flood or other inevitable accident.[126] There is also an exemption for unfitness caused by the contract-holder or a permitted occupier.[127]

There is no obligation on a landlord to deal with fitness issues unless they become "aware that works or repairs are necessary". If there is more than one landlord then the knowledge of any one of them is sufficient.[128] This is a little different from the existing position which requires the landlord

---

[123] In Schedule 1 to the Housing Health and Safety Rating System (Wales) Regulations 2006.

[124] See the guidance to the standard at: www.gov.uk/government/publications/a-decent-home-definition-and-guidance.

[125] Introduced by the Homes (Fitness for Human Habitation) Act 2018.

[126] RHWA, s95.

[127] RWHA, s96.

[128] RHWA, s97.

to be on notice of a need to repair, at least within premises which are demised to a tenant, and to have no liability where this notice has not been given.[129] How this position is to square with the language used in the RHWA is less clear. It seems likely that explicit notice of a fitness issue is not required and a landlord must merely be aware of the need. Added to this is the additional element that if a landlord buys a property they are also deemed to have knowledge of any fitness issues the previous landlord was aware of. This is likely to be a matter that conveyancers will wish to consider and they will want to seek confirmation from a vendor that they are not aware of any fitness problems.

Repairing Obligations

The RHWA has essentially re-enacted existing repairing obligations found in residential leases.[130] However, it has sought to codify a number of points that were formerly dealt with in the case law. The basic obligations remain unchanged. That is to:

- keep in repair the structure and exterior including the drains, gutters and external pipes; and

- keep in repair and proper working order the installations for the supply of water, gas or electricity, sanitation, space heating, and hot water.

The standard of repair is whatever is reasonable considering the age and character of the property, and the period during which it is likely to be available for occupation as a home. Where the property is part of a building there is also an obligation to keep in repair parts of the building in which the landlord has an estate or interest or which he owns or

---

[129] *Edwards v Kumarasamy* [2016] UKSC 40.

[130] In s11, Landlord and Tenant Act 1985.

controls.[131] That obligation however does not require work to be done unless the disrepair or failure to keep in proper working order affects the contract-holder's enjoyment of the dwelling, or other common parts that they are entitled to make use of.[132]

These obligations are much the same as the existing legislation and so the case law on interpreting the scope of these obligations and the standard of repair required will continue to be relevant.

There is no scope to contract out of the repairing obligations in leases of less than seven years. Although this is not formally expressed in the legislation the repairing obligations are described as fundamental terms and so are automatically in every occupation-contract with a restriction on their amendment as a result. That said, while a technical right to contract out of repairing obligations with court permission exists in the historic repairing obligations,[133] it is almost never used in any event.

As with fitness there is no obligation to carry out repairs where the want of repair was caused by fire, storm, flood or other inevitable accident. However, the exemption for fitness which allows for work to be avoided where it cannot be carried out at reasonable expense has no application in relation to the obligation to repair.[134] There is also an exemption for repairs caused by the contract-holder or a permitted occupier failing to take proper care of the property.[135]

Again, as with fitness, there is no obligation to repair unless the landlord become "aware that works or repairs are necessary". If there is more than one landlord then the knowledge of any one of them is sufficient. The

---

[131] RHWA, s91.

[132] RHWA, s95(5).

[133] S12, Landlord and Tenant Act 1985.

[134] RHWA, s95.

[135] RWHA, s96.

same position on sale by one landlord to another also applies.[136] There is a supplementary provision, however, which obliges a contract-holder to notify the landlord where they become aware of any "fault, defect, damage or disrepair" which they believe is for the landlord to resolve.[137]

Electrical Safety

The RHWA has sought to catch-up a bit with England which has had a requirement on residential landlords to provide electrical safety certificates for some time.[138] In Wales, this was imposed via regulations as a fitness test. There is no enforcement by local authorities, as there is in England, and no civil penalties. Instead, a property in Wales is deemed to be unfit for human habitation if a landlord does not have the proper electrical certifications.[139]

The regulations require that a landlord has a valid electrical condition report in place at all times. This is a report from an appropriately qualified person which sets out that the installation is safe. That report must be repeated every five years or at such shorter interval as is specified in the report. That report must be given to the contract holder within 14 days of the occupation date.[140] If the report is renewed when the contract holder is in place then the new report must be given within 14 days.

---

[136] RHWA, s97.

[137] Regulation 14 of the Renting Homes (Supplementary Provisions) (Wales) Regulations 2022.

[138] Through the Electrical Safety Standards in the Private Rented Sector (England) Regulations 2020.

[139] Regulation 6(6) of the Renting Homes (Fitness for Human Habitation) (Wales) Regulations 2022.

[140] All timelines relating to electrical safety were increased from seven days to 14 days by regulation 2 of the Renting Homes (Fitness for Human

If the electrical report requires investigation or remediation work then the property will not be fit for human habitation until that is done. The contract holder must be provided with a copy of the confirmation of the work within 14 days of the landlord receiving that confirmation.[141]

If a landlord has breached any element of the electrical regulation then he can resolve the position late by obtaining and/or providing the report to the contract holder.[142]

In relation to converted tenancies there is a period of 12 months from 1 December 2022 to comply by obtaining the necessary electrical report.[143] Any report done before 1 December 2022 will be valid for the period marked on that report or five years from its date of obtaining.

Smoke and CO Alarms

Wales has also sought to catch up with England which requires smoke and carbon monoxide alarms[144] by specifying that a property is not fit for human habitation without them.[145]

Landlord must have a working smoke alarm on each storey of their property. These alarms must be connected to the mains electricity and must be connected to any other alarms. There must also be a working

---

Habitation) (Wales) (Amendment) Regulations 2022 shortly before the RHWA came into effect.

[141] Regulation 6(5).

[142] Regulation 6(7).

[143] Regulation 7(2).

[144] The Smoke and Carbon Monoxide Alarm (England) Regulations 2015 amended by the Smoke and Carbon Monoxide Alarm (Amendment) Regulations 2022.

[145] Regulation 5 of the Renting Homes (Fitness for Human Habitation) (Wales) Regulations 2022.

carbon monoxide alarm in any room containing a gas appliance (including a gas oven or cooker) and any oil or solid fuel burning appliance.

Landlords can fix their position by installing functional alarms at any time and the property will be fit for human habitation at the point this is done.

For converted contracts there is a period of 12 months from 1 December 2022 to achieve compliance with the smoke alarm requirement. There is no time for compliance with the CO alarm obligation and all properties in Wales that are subject to the RHWA must have the necessary alarms in place as from 1 December 2022.

Gas Safety

The RHWA has no gas safety provisions of its own. The existing gas safety requirements applying to landlords will continue to apply in Wales under the RHWA with no notable changes.[146]

Breach of Obligations

There is nothing specifically in the RHWA as to the precise damages to be awarded against a landlord in breach of an obligation. Therefore, existing case law on damages is likely to continue to apply and there will be a payment relating to the loss of the amenity value to the contract-holder. There are far better and more complete analyses of this case law that are more appropriate to consult in this regard.

There is no case law in relation to fitness at the time of writing. However, if a property is unfit for human habitation then it seems that its amenity value to a contract-holder must be close to zero. A landlord might be able

---

[146] Regulation 36 of the Gas Safety (Installation and Use) Regulations 1998.

to argue that there is a residual value in providing storage for a contract-holder's possessions but it would be hard to claim much more benefit than this.

There is a supplemental term which specifies that contract-holders are not liable to pay rent in respect or each day or part-day during which a property is not fit for habitation. However, this is a supplemental term and so landlords can freely delete it from an occupation contract.[147]

There are also express provisions under the RHWA which allow a court to order specific performance of a landlords repairing and fitness obligations which override any equitable limit on those rights.[148]

Additionally, the RHWA extends the right to enforce breaches of repairing or fitness obligations beyond the contract-holder and allows permitted occupiers of the property to enforce loss or damage claims against the landlord provided they were permitted to reside in the property.[149]

Removal of tenant obligations

Finally, the RHWA has eliminated the doctrines of waste and the implied obligation on a tenant to use a property in a tenant-like manner.[150] These obligations are largely replaced with supplemental terms but which are again subject to amendment or removal.[151] There is an exception for

---

[147] Regulation 11 of the Renting Homes (Supplementary Provisions) (Wales) Regulations 2022.

[148] RHWA, s100.

[149] RHWA, s99.

[150] RHWA, s101.

[151] Regulation 13 of the Renting Homes (Supplementary Provisions) (Wales) Regulations 2022.

converted contracts and the doctrines of waste and tenant-like use continue to apply in relation to converted contracts.[152]

Rights of Access

Landlord have a right of access to a property at any reasonable time to either inspect its condition and state of repair or to carry out works for which they are liable but they must give 24 hour's notice of their intention to exercise the right.[153] There is also a supplemental term permitting a landlord to access the property on the same basis if a contract-holder has not complied with any obligation on them to repair things that are not the responsibility of the landlord so that the landlord can carry out that repair.[154] There is a further supplemental term which permits a landlord to demand immediate access in the case of an emergency. That term further allows a landlord to access the property themselves if immediate access is not provided but they must use all reasonable endeavours to tell the contract-holder that they have done so as soon as the reasonably can.[155] This would seem to sit poorly with the right to quiet enjoyment but that right has been carefully qualified under the RHWA and it is not breached if a landlord reasonable exercises their rights under the occupation-contract.[156]

---

[152] RHWA, Schedule 12, para 16.

[153] RHWA, s98.

[154] Regulation 15 of the Renting Homes (Supplementary Provisions) (Wales) Regulations 2022.

[155] Regulation 16 of the Renting Homes (Supplementary Provisions) (Wales) Regulations 2022.

[156] RHWA, s54(2).

CHAPTER EIGHT

RENT

The RHWA makes some substantial changes to the manner in which rent is handled. In fact, it seems to radically reduce the protections available to contract holders.

Rent cannot be varied during a fixed term tenancy. However, there appears to be no control within the legislation as to the level it is set at. This is a surprise in that existing private sector tenancies are controlled such that rent cannot be above the market level and if the rent is above that level it can be referred to a tribunal for determination. No such similar provision is available in the RHWA. Presumably, the expectation is that market forces will prevent rents being set above the market level.

During a periodic tenancy rent can be varied.[157] There is no restriction on the amount it can be increased by or how soon this can happen after a tenancy commences, even in secure contracts.[158] The only requirements are that at least two months' notice of the increase must be given and the prescribed form must be used. The form is the same regardless of contract type.[159] The notice is not required to expire on any particular date and the only other restriction is once the rent has been increased then the rent cannot be increased for one year after the date on which the last increase came into effect. In other words, a further notice can be served ten months after the increase on the last notice became effective so that the rent increases after twelve months. There is no provision in the legislation for a rent increase to be challenged.

---

[157] RHWA, s123.

[158] RHWA, s104.

[159] Form RHW12.

This seems an odd structure to adopt. To some extent, it seems to have been felt that existing case law would solve many problems. For example, during evidence the Senedd committee considering the bill that would become the RHWA had its attention drawn to a Court of Appeal decision which held that a rent increase clause which massively increased the rent in a tenancy from around £4,500 to £25,000 (eliminating the statutory protection at that time) was a sham as it was a device to avoid statutory protection.[160] This decision led the Senedd committee to the view that there was no need for specific anti-avoidance provisions to prevent clauses doubling the rent as a means to force tenants out.

However, that decision applied to a clause in a contract not a statutory increase made according to the law. Therefore, it would seem to be open to a landlord under the RHWA to increase the rent using the statutory process such that the rent essentially becomes unaffordable to a contract holder. While the court may reject a massive increase such as seen in previous cases, it would be far harder to deal with an increase that pushed the rent to a figure a little above the market rate which would be potentially unaffordable to many occupiers and would essentially serve to push them out.

It is less clear from the legislation if rent increase clauses can be placed in fixed term and periodic contracts and whether a clause in a fixed term contract continues in a periodic contract. In similar situations in tenancies under the Housing Act 1988 it was held that a rent increase clause in a fixed term tenancy did not survive into a periodic tenancy.[161] However, the wording in the legislation as to the manner in which clauses in fixed term tenancies are ported into periodic tenancies is very different from the way that clauses in fixed-term standard contracts are ported into periodic standard contracts.[162] The Welsh version of the tenant fees

---

[160] *Bankway Properties Ltd v Dunsford & Anor* [2001] EWCA Civ 528.

[161] *London District Properties Management Ltd & Ors v Goolamy & Anor* [2009] EWHC 1367

[162] RHWA, s184.

legislation has specific provisions allowing for rent increase clauses.[163] Given that this legislation was written when the RHWA had already been passed, albeit that it was not in force, and it continues unchanged into the life of the RHWA it is clear that the drafter of the legislation, and presumably the Senedd, were of the view that rent increase clauses were possible in the RHWA otherwise there would have been little purpose in legislating to control them.

The decision not to have any specific provisions to allow for rent to be contested is all the more surprising when one bears in mind that where a contract has been converted from a Housing Act 1988 tenancy the power to increase the rent under that legislation has been re-enacted for those converted contracts.[164] However, it is subject to the same controls as it would have been under a Housing Act 1988 tenancy, in other words the contract-holder may refer the proposed rent increase to the relevant Welsh rent assessment committee for them to determine an appropriate market rent in accordance with the assumptions set out in the relevant regulation.[165]

---

[163] Renting Homes (Fees etc.) (Wales) Act 2019, Schedule 1, para 1.

[164] Renting Homes (Rent Determination) (Converted Contracts) (Wales) Regulations 2022 as amended by the Renting Homes (Rent Determination) (Converted Contracts) (Wales) (Amendment) Regulations 2022.

[165] Regulation 6 of the Renting Homes (Rent Determination) (Converted Contracts) (Wales) Regulations 2022 (as amended).

CHAPER NINE

TERM AND POSSESSION

Possession Without Specific Cause

For standard contracts there is a power to terminate without specific reasons that is analogous to the previous possession on notice found in Assured Shorthold Tenancies.[166] However, the scope of the notice is much more limited.[167] A landlord cannot give notice inside a fixed term standard contract, except in limited cases with a break clause, only in a periodic standard contract. In addition, notice cannot be given in the first six months after the initial occupation of the property by the contract-holder.[168] If the occupation contract is a replacement for a previous contract between the same landlord and contract-holder for the same property then the six-month minimum occupancy period is counted from the start of the original occupation contract. The notice period cannot be less than six months save in a small range of specified circumstances.[169] In practice, therefore a standard contract holder will be assured of not less than 12 months in their property unless they breach some term of the agreement. Essentially this was part of the policy drive of the Welsh Government in the RHWA to increase the length of occupations in Wales. There is a form for the giving of notice which should be used.[170]

---

[166] Under s21, Housing Act 1988.

[167] RHWA, s173.

[168] RHWA, s175.

[169] RHWA, s174.

[170] Form RHW16.

While it is not normally possible to give notice to expire at the end of the fixed term of a standard contract there are a limited range of cases where that is in fact possible. These are:

- Occupation contracts which would not have been an occupation contract but have become one because notice was given before the occupation;

- Supported standard contracts;

- Standard contracts made to provide accommodation for asylum seekers or homeless people;

- Service occupancies where the contract holder is occupying the property as part of their employment;

- Standard contracts provided for members of the police or fire service as part of their employment;

- Temporary accommodation where the land has been acquired for development purposes;

- Temporary accommodation where the property has been let to the landlord so that they can provide temporary housing and that superior lease contains a provision allowing the landlord to end the lease on notice;

- Accommodation provided by the landlord to the contract holder as a temporary expedient while works are being carried out on the property previously occupied by the contract holder and the landlord of the temporary property is not the same as the landlord of the previously occupied property.

As usual there is a specific prescribed form for giving notice in these situations.[171]

There are also a range of further restrictions on giving notice, which are not dissimilar to those that have been applied in England.[172] So a landlord cannot give notice where:[173]

- They have not supplied the contract-holder with a proper written statement and if it is provided late for six months from the date it is provided;

- They have not provided a notice setting out their address details;

- They have not complied with the Energy Performance regulations;[174]

- They have failed to comply with their deposit obligations;

- They have taken a payment prohibited by the tenant fee legislation;[175]

- There are no or insufficient working smoke and carbon monoxide alarms installed;

- They have not got a valid EICR;

---

[171] Form RHW22.

[172] By way of the changes made by the Deregulation Act 2015.

[173] RHWA, Schedule 9A.

[174] Being the Energy Performance of Buildings (England and Wales) Regulations 2012.

[175] Renting Homes (Fees etc.) (Wales) Act 2019.

- They have not got a valid gas safety certificate.

However, there are critical differences from England in that all of these situations can be fixed. A landlord without a gas safety certificate can get one for example, which in England cannot be fixed if one did not exist before the tenant occupied to the property.[176]

As is also now found in England these notices have a time limit by which they must be used. Where a notice has been given then court proceedings for possession must be commenced within two months from the date for possession given in the notice. This means that if the landlord, for whatever reason, gives more than six months' notice of his desire to seek possession then that does not alter the amount of time that he has to commence proceedings.[177] The language used in England and Wales differs however. In England the legislation states that proceedings "may not be begun after the end of the period of six months" from the date the notice was served.[178] The RHWA states that the landlord "may not make a possession claim ... after the end of the period of two months" of the expiry date in the notice. In England, it has been found that the use of the work "begun" means issued and that specifically means processed, stamped, and served by the court. This has been an increasing problem in the current era of growing court delays. Despite the Civil Procedure Rules stating that a claim is "brought" at the date it is received in the court office for the purposes of "the Limitation Act 1980 and any other relevant statute" the Court of Appeal has held that this is distinct from the use of the word begun and so a landlord who delivers his possession papers to the court in good time in England but then falls foul of the time limits as a result of the court's own tardiness is still out of time.[179]

---

[176] *Trecarrell House Ltd v Rouncefield* [2020] EWCA Civ

[177] RHWA, s179.

[178] S21(4D), Housing Act 1988.

[179] *Salford CC v Garner* [2004] EWCA Civ 364

Whether the same reasoning would apply in Wales with the different wording is uncertain.

There are also further restrictions where a notice has been given but is either withdrawn, not used, or is defective. A landlord can withdraw a possession notice within 28 days from it being given using the prescribed form.[180] The notice can be withdrawn later than the 28-day limit but the contract-holder must either agree to that or must object within a reasonable time period.[181]

If the notice is withdrawn by the landlord then there is a period of 28 days from the date of withdrawal to give one further notice after which point there is no ability to give a further notice of this type for six months from the date of withdrawal. Likewise if a landlord does not issue proceedings for possession within the two month period permitted by the RHWA then the same six month limit on serving a further notice with the start of that period being the last day on which proceedings could have been issued.[182] This means that landlords who realise that they have served a defective notice have a limited opportunity to fix that issue if they withdraw it. Equally, a landlord who delays issuing proceedings and loses their opportunity is essentially unable to have a further try for several months. However, the RHWA is less than clear on this issue. While there is a restriction which states specifically that if a notice is withdrawn then there is a period before a fresh one can be issued there is nothing specifically in the legislation which states that a landlord cannot in fact issue multiple notices without withdrawing them. The common law position has always been that serving a second or subsequent notice to terminate a tenancy does not render the first notice, or any of the others invalid.[183] As there is no specific provision in the RHWA that prohibits multiple notices or suggests that any of them are

---

[180] Form RHW19.

[181] RHWA, s180.

[182] RHWA, s177.

[183] *Lowenthal v Vanhoute & Anor* [1947] KB 342.

invalid then, as long as a notice is not formally withdrawn, it appears that multiple notices are possible.

Break Clauses

Contractual break clauses allowing for the termination of a fixed term tenancy without a specific cause are tightly controlled under the RHWA.[184] A break clause is only permitted in a fixed term standard contract where the term is for more than two years or if it falls into one of the listed exceptions.[185] These are similar to the exceptions which apply to other types of notice without cause include where:

- Occupation contracts which would not have been an occupation contract but have become one because notice was given before the occupation;

- Supported standard contracts;

- Standard contracts made to provide accommodation for asylum seekers or homeless people;

- Service occupancies where the contract holder is occupying the property as part of their employment;

- Standard contracts provided for members of the police or fire service as part of their employment;

- Temporary accommodation where the land has been acquired for development purposes;

---

[184] RHWA, s194.

[185] RHWA, Schedule 9C.

- Temporary accommodation where the property has been let to the landlord so that they can provide temporary housing and that superior lease contains a provision allowing the landlord to end the lease on notice;

- Accommodation provided by the landlord to the contract holder as a temporary expedient while works are being carried out on the property previously occupied by the contract holder and the landlord of the temporary property is not the same as the landlord of the previously occupied property.

A break notice must give at least six months' notice save in specific cases[186] which allow for two months' notice.[187] Notice cannot be given during the first 18 months. In practice this means that for any break clause to be worthwhile the fixed term tenancy must be for considerably longer than two years.

All the same restrictions[188] and time limits[189] on giving notice without cause in a periodic standard contract apply equally in relation to notices under a break clause. There is also a prescribed form for use when giving notice in accordance with a break clause.[190]

Shorter Notice Periods

While in most cases a landlord must give six months' notice when they are seeking to give notice without any specific reason there are limited range of cases where notice can be given which is only for two months.

---

[186] In RHWA, Schedule 8A.

[187] RHWA, s195 and s195A.

[188] RHWA, s197 and s198.

[189] RHWA, s200.

[190] Form RHW24.

Again, they are not dissimilar to other exceptions to the rules for these notice types.[191] These shorter notice periods have their own forms for giving notice.[192] These are where the occupation contract is:

- A prohibited conduct standard contract;

- For a tenancies or licences which are only occupation contracts because of notice because they are for holiday accommodation, care institutions, temporary expedients, or shared accommodation;

- A standard contract provided by a landlord who is a higher education institution to a contract-holder for the purpose of them attending a course of study;

- A supported standard contract;

- A standard contract made for providing accommodation as support for asylum seekers;

- A standard contract made to provide accommodation for the homeless;

- A standard contract where the contract-holder is required by his or her contract of employment to occupy the dwelling and for police or fire service staff whose accommodation is provided as part of their employment;

- A standard contract provided for temporary accommodation where the land has been acquired for development.

---

[191] RHWA, Schedule 8A.

[192] Form RHW17 or from RHW18 for introductory standard contracts or prohibited conduct standard contracts.

- A standard contract where the dwelling has been let to the landlord with vacant possession for use as temporary housing accommodation and the lease includes a provision for the superior landlord to obtain vacant possession from the landlord at the end of a specified period or when required;

- A standard contract where the dwelling has been provided to the contract-holder by a different landlord while works are carried out on the dwelling previously occupied by the contract-holder.

There is also a specific exemption for converted contracts which were previously Assured Shorthold Tenancies under the Housing Act 1988. For those contracts the prior right to give two months' notice at the end of any fixed term or in a periodic tenancy[193] is preserved.[194] There is a specific prescribed form for giving notice in this situation.[195] However, the ability to give notice in this way has been time-limited by last minute amendments to the RHWA[196] such that the period during which two months' notice can be given under a converted Assured Shorthold Tenancy is just six months from the date the RHWA came into force, that is prior to 1 June 2023.

There are also exceptions to the inability to give notice without cause in the first six months of an occupation contract or inside the first 18 months of an occupation contract where there is reliance on a break clause.[197] Again these are similar to the exceptions for other notices of this style and are where the occupation contract is:

---

[193] Under s21, Housing Act 1988.

[194] RHWA, Schedule 12, para 25A inserted by the Renting Homes (Amendment) (Wales) Act 2021.

[195] Form RHW38.

[196] By the Renting Homes (Wales) Act 2016 (Amendment of Schedule 12 and Consequential Amendment) Regulations 2022.

[197] RHWA, Schedule 9.

- A prohibited conduct standard contract;

- For a tenancies or licences which are only occupation contracts because of notice because they are for holiday accommodation, care institutions, temporary expedients, or shared accommodation;

- A standard contract provided by a landlord who is a higher education institution to a contract-holder for the purpose of them attending a course of study;

- A supported standard contract;

- A standard contract made for providing accommodation as support for asylum seekers;

- A standard contract made to provide accommodation for the homeless;

- A standard contract where the contract-holder is required by his or her contract of employment to occupy the dwelling and for police or fire service staff whose accommodation is provided as part of their employment;

- A standard contract provided for temporary accommodation where the land has been acquired for development.

- A standard contract where the dwelling has been let to the landlord with vacant possession for use as temporary housing accommodation and the lease includes a provision for the superior landlord to obtain vacant possession from the landlord at the end of a specified period or when required;

- A standard contract where the dwelling has been provided to the contract-holder by a different landlord while works are carried out on the dwelling previously occupied by the contract-holder.

All of these various exceptions are subject to variation by regulations made by the Welsh Ministers. Therefore while they might all be very similar initially it is quite possible that they will diverge over time.

Converted Contracts

In relation to converted contracts which were previously Assured Shorthold Tenancies then there are specific and in some cases time-limited exceptions. For these standard contracts the landlord's right to give two months' notice of their desire to seek possession without cause expiring either at the end of the fixed term tenancy or thereafter is retained.[198] There is a specific form for this notice.[199]

In addition, if a contract is periodic and was an Assured Shorthold Tenancy before conversion the notice period is reduced from six months to two months.[200] However, less than an hour before the RHWA came into force regulations were passed to limit the ability to give this notice up to six months after the date the RHWA came into force, that is to 1 June 2023.[201]

---

[198] RHWA, Schedule 12, para 25B.

[199] Form RHW38.

[200] RHWA, Schedule 12, para 25A.

[201] Regulation 5 of the Renting Homes (Wales) Act 2016 (Amendment of Schedule 12 and Consequential Amendment) Regulations 2022.

For fully assured tenancies that have become standard contracts by conversion then the provisions on giving notice without cause are disapplied, protecting tenant's previous rights.[202]

Retaliation

In any case where a landlord under a standard contract is seeking to recover possession on the basis of a notice which does not require a specific reason to be given for possession[203] then the court is able to refuse a possession order if they believe the possession claim is retaliatory.[204] A claim is retaliatory if a contract holder has required a landlord to comply with their obligations to keep the property in repair or make it free for human habitation[205] and the court is satisfied that the landlord is seeking possession to avoid complying with those obligations. Notably there is nothing that prevents a landlord doing the repairs sought and then seeking possession provided they are not evicting to avoid repairing and are doing it as a genuine act of retaliation! The Welsh Ministers can add further actions which are deemed to be retaliatory by regulations but have not done so at the time of writing.

As well as the possibility of a possession claim being dismissed on the basis of retaliation there is a further restriction on future possession claims. If a court refuses to give possession on the basis that the notice is retaliatory then no further notice of the same type can be given for six months from the date that the court made the order that the notice was

---

[202] RHWA, Schedule 12, para 25.

[203] That is a notice given under s173 or s194.

[204] RHWA, s217.

[205] The obligations under s91 or 92, RHWA.

retaliatory in nature.[206] Therefore it is not possible for a landlord to simply serve another notice and go back to court.

Breach of Contract

In any case where a contract-holder breaches a term of an occupation contract then possession can be made on that basis.[207] The appropriate prescribed form[208] must be served first and the contract-holder is entitled to one month of notice before proceedings are commenced. Proceedings must be commenced within six months of giving the notice.[209] The court may only make an order for possession if it considers it reasonable to do so.[210]

False Statements

In any situation where a false statement is made "knowingly or recklessly", by the contract-holder or by someone else acting at their instigation and this induces a landlord to make an occupation contract then this is deemed to be a breach of contract and a landlord can make a possession claim on that basis.[211] The wording in this section is analogous to similar wording in pre-cursor legislation and so it is likely that existing case law would apply to it.[212] So although it is a question of

---

[206] RHWA, s177A. Inserted by the Renting Homes (Amendment) (Wales) Act 2021.

[207] RHWA, s157.

[208] Form RHW23.

[209] RHWA, s159.

[210] RHWA, s209.

[211] RHWA, s158.

[212] Ground 17, Schedule 2, Housing Act 1988 and Ground 5, Schedule 2, Housing Act 1985.

reasonableness as to whether to make an order for possession, a deliberate lie to obtain a contract should lead to a possession order other than in exceptional circumstances.[213] Where possession is being sought due to someone else telling lies at the contract-holder's instigation then it must be shown that the contract-holder actively urged or incited that false statement rather than merely benefitting from it.[214]

Estate Management Grounds

A landlord can make a claim for possession on one or more of the estate management grounds, although these are not all available to every landlord in every contract type.[215] The grounds are:[216]

Ground	Title	Summary
A	Building works	The landlord intends to demolish or reconstruct the property or a building containing it or to carry out works and this cannot be done without possession
B	Redevelopment scheme	The property or part of it is in an area of an approved redevelopment scheme and the landlord intends to sell as part of that scheme
C	Charities	The landlord is and has all times been a charity and the continued occupation would conflict with the charitable objects

---

[213] *Shrewsbury and Atcham BC v Evans* (1998) 30 H.L.R. 123.

[214] *Merton LBC v Richards* [2005] EWCA Civ 639.

[215] RHWA, s160.

[216] RHWA, Schedule 8, part 1

D	Dwelling suitable for disabled people	The property has features designed for the occupation of disabled people, no such person is occupying it anymore and the landlord requires the property for that use
E	People difficult to house	The landlord is a housing association or trust which houses people who are difficult to house and there is no such person living at the property anymore or they have been offered other accommodation and the property is needed for that purpose
F	Groups of dwellings for people with special needs	The property is part of a group of properties for people with special needs, services are provided nearby for that purpose, no such person is living there anymore, and the property is required for such a person
G	Reserve successor	The contract-holder was a reserve successor and the property is larger than they reasonably need
H	Joint contract-holders	The contract-holder was a joint contract-holder and another joint contract-holder has left the accommodation and the property is now larger than the remaining contract-holder or holders need or the remaining contract-holders do not meet a community landlord's allocation criteria

I	Other estate management grounds	Some other substantial estate management reason means that the landlord should obtain possession

The court must consider it reasonable to give possession and must also be satisfied that suitable alternative accommodation will be available for the contract-holder.[217] In addition, if a possession order is made on any of the grounds other than ground A or B then the landlord must pay the contract-holder's reasonable probable moving expenses.[218] Note that the provision simply requires payment of the "likely" moving expenses as opposed to the actual expenses and so it seems an estimate is permitted. A notice must be given in the appropriate prescribed form[219] and must give at least one month's notice. Possession actions must be commenced before the date six months from the date the notice was served. If there is reliance on the redevelopment scheme ground (ground B) then the notice can be served before all the conditions of that scheme have been met. If the notice is relying on the ground relating to successors who do not need such large accommodation (ground G) then it cannot be given until at least six months after the landlord became aware of the death of the previous contract-holder and must be given before the end of twelve months from that same point. If there is reliance on grounds relating to departing joint contract-holders (ground H) then notice must be given before the date which is six months after that joint contract-holders rights were ended.[220]

---

[217] RHWA, s210.

[218] RHWA, s160(4).

[219] Form RHW23.

[220] RHWA, s161.

Reasonableness

In all the possession scenarios in which a consideration of reasonableness is required the RHWA has departed from the existing case law and has set out in some detail how reasonableness is to be dealt with.[221] Notably the wording of the RHWA copies that of some of its predecessors and suggests that even if the ground of reasonableness is met then the court still has a discretion as to whether or not the order is made as the RHWA states that a court "may not" make an order unless it considers it reasonable to do so but it in no way specifies that the court "must" make such an order even if it does consider it reasonable. In fact, the new wording does not really make a huge change in the existing accepted structure of reasonableness in that it requires the court to carry out a balancing test between the effect on the contract-holder of making the decision as against the effect on the landlord of not making one. The RHWA does also bring in the need to consider third parties as well such as other contract-holders of the landlord, neighbours, and those seeking accommodation from that landlord and it will be interesting to see the extent to which the court has regard to those additional parties and what that means for its decision-making.

In relation to any breach of contract or estate management possession claim the court has an unfettered power to adjourn proceedings to a later date if it considers it reasonable to do so. It can also postpone any possession order by suspending it or staying the execution of it for any period of time it considers fit. Any adjournment may also include conditions requiring the contract-holder to pay arrears of rent or to pay the rent going forward and can also impose any other conditions it considers appropriate. If those conditions are complied with the court can also discharge the possession order altogether. When considering reasonableness of adjournment or suspension the same considerations are

---

[221] RHWA, Schedule 10.

appropriate as for considering whether to make the order in the first place.[222]

Rent Arrears

Termination for arrears of rent is possible in all occupation contracts but by way of a breach of contract claim. However, for standard contracts there is a specific statutory right to possession associated with serious rent arrears.[223] Possession for serious rent arrears is very similar to the ground for possession in the pre-cursor of the standard contract.[224] This allows for possession where:

- at least eight weeks' rent is unpaid for contracts with a rental period of a week, a fortnight or four weeks;

- at least two months' rent is unpaid for contracts with rental period of a month;

- at least one quarter's rent is more than three months in arrears for rental periods which are quarterly;

- at least 25% of the rent is more than three months in arrears if the rental period is yearly.

As with previous systems the consideration of arrears is at two points in time only, at the time the notice is served and at the time the court hears the possession claim.[225] The landlord must serve the appropriate form on

---

[222] RHWA, s211.

[223] RHWA, s181 for periodic standard contracts and s187 for fixed term standard contracts.

[224] Ground 8, Schedule 2, Housing Act 1988.

[225] RHWA, s216.

the contract-holder[226] and must give at least 14 days notice of the commencement of proceedings. The proceedings must be commenced within six months of service o the notice.[227]

Other Defences

There are blanket defences in all possession actions that there is a breach of the contract-holders rights under the European Convention on Human Rights. There is also an ability to ask the court to review the original decision to take possession proceedings if the landlord is a community landlord or it is otherwise subject to judicial review.[228] This effectively creates a new judicial review jurisdiction of a limited sort within the county court.

Death

Contracts end if there is a sole contract-holder and that contract-holder dies. The contract ends automatically one month after the death of the contract-holder or earlier if the landlord is given notice of the death by the contract-holders personal representatives or all the permitted occupiers of the dwelling.[229] If the contract is a licence then the death of the landlord also brings it to an end.[230] This is one of the few areas where the RHWA recognises a distinction between tenancies and licences and utilises it.

---

[226] Form RHW20 or RHW21 for Introductory or Prohibited Conduct Standard Contracts

[227] RHWA, s182 and s188.

[228] RHWA, s218.

[229] RHWA, s155.

[230] RHWA, s156.

Anti-Social Behaviour and Exclusion

The RHWA does not provide for specific eviction for anti-social behaviour as such. It has provisions in relation to joint contract-holders and it also includes anti-social behaviour restrictions as a fundamental term, so allowing for eviction for breach of that term but there is no specific right to evict for ASB as there is for serious rent arrears. However, there is a right to evict on short notice as there is in pre-cursor legislation.[231] Where a notice is given of the intention to commence proceedings for possession for a breach of contract, in contrast to the normal requirement of one month's notice, it is permitted to give notice stating that possession proceedings will begin the same day where there is reliance on ASB.[232] Interestingly, unlike in previous legislation there is nothing clear in the statutory language that allows other breaches to ride along with this shorter notice period[233] and so if a claim was to be made for rent arrears as well it seem that this would require a separate notice giving the usual one month warning.

However the RHWA has a radical new power for use in relation to specific contract types, that is the power of exclusion. In relation to supported standard contracts the landlord is empowered to require a contract-holder who it reasonably believes has:

- Used violence against any person in the property;

- Done anything in the property which carries a significant risk of harm to another person; or

---

[231] Such as under ground 14, Schedule 2, Housing Act 1988.

[232] RHWA, s159(2).

[233] See s8(4), Housing Act 1988.

- Behaved in such a way that it impedes another resident of the supported accommodation from benefitting from the support being provided;

Then there is a right to serve a notice in the appropriate prescribed form[234] to exclude that person from the property for a period of up to 48 hours. This power cannot be used more often than three times in any six-month period starting from the first period of exclusion.[235] The Welsh ministers are obliged to issue guidance on the use of this power[236] and they have done so.[237] Landlords are obliged to have regard to that guidance. This power is extremely troubling. Unlike possession actions there is no power built into the RHWA to seek a review of this decision, whether by the landlord or through the courts. Therefore the only recourse for someone faced with an exclusion would be to launch an urgent judicial review. In practice, the exclusion period would likely be over before that could be dealt with by the courts. The people subject to exclusions are some of the most vulnerable occupiers in Wales and so it seems dangerous to potentially make them subject to exclusion without any means of challenging that. This is even more troubling when the form used to notify these people of the exclusion is considered. It contains no information telling them that there is guidance their landlord must follow, or any information suggesting that they might be able to challenge the decision or how to go about doing so. In a piece of legislation that has as a driving force increasing the rights of occupiers these provisions seem like a seriously retrograde step.

---

[234] Form RHW15.

[235] RHWA, s145.

[236] RHWA, s146.

[237] Available at https://www.gov.wales/renting-homes-supported-accommodation.

Repudiatory Breaches

If a landlord commits a repudiatory breach of the contract and the contract-holder gives up possession due to that breach then the contract ends at that point.[238] This does not in any way specify what might be a repudiatory breach. Indeed, the case law on the issue is at best chequered and it has never been definitively decided by the courts that a repudiatory breach can end a tenancy.[239] Clearly, the RHWA resolves that question but it remains that case that the only case law which sets out what might in fact be repudiatory breach is serious disrepair.[240]

Agreements

Unsurprisingly, the RHWA also allows for contracts to be terminated by agreement as long as the contract-holder leaves the property in accordance with that agreement.[241]

Joint Contract-Holders

There are a range of provisions that allow for joint contract-holders to end or transfer their status under contracts that they share with others. Landlords also have powers to end the rights of a single joint contract-holder without ending the entire contract.

Where a landlord believes that a joint contract-holder is not occupying a property and does not intend to occupy it they can give notice in the prescribed form[242] to that joint contract-holder telling them of their

---

[238] RHWA, s154.

[239] See the discussion in *Reichman v Beveridge* [2006] EWCA Civ 1659.

[240] *Hussein v Mehlman* [1992] 2 EGLR 287.

[241] RHWA, s153.

[242] Form RHW29.

intention to end their contract. This notice must also be given to every other joint contract-holder. This is only possible of the contract expressly states that the contract-holder must occupy the property as their only or principal home. Over the next four weeks the landlord must make enquiries to satisfy themselves that the contract-holder is not occupying the property and has no intention to do so. At the end of the four weeks the landlord may serve a second notice on the joint contract-holder with copies to the other contract-holders in the property, again using the relevant prescribed form.[243] Eight weeks after the service of that second notice the contract in respect of that joint contract-holder comes to an end. It continues for the remaining contract-holders unaffected.[244] At any point during the eight weeks after the service of the second notice the affected contract-holder may apply to the court on the basis that either:

- They were not given the first warning notice;

- They did occupy or intend to occupy the property and they had good reasons for not responding to the warning notice; or

- The landlord had no reasonable grounds for believing that the contract-holder did not occupy and intend to occupy the property at the time the second notice was served.

The court may effectively quash the notice so that the contract-holder remains a party to the occupation contract and make any such other order it sees fit.[245]

In a similar vein one joint contract-holder can serve notice on another joint contract-holder on the basis that despite being required to occupy the property as a home they are not doing so and do not intend to do so.

---

[243] Form RHW30.

[244] RHWA, s225.

[245] RHWA, s226.

This notice has a prescribed form.[246] It must be served on the contract-holder believed not to be occupying the property, every other joint contract-holder (if any), and to the landlord. There is then a four-week holding period during which the complaining contract-holder must make enquiries to establish if the original contract-holder does not occupy or intend to occupy the property. At the end of that period the complaining contract-holder may apply to the court to have the original contract-holder removed from the contract. They will be removed as from the date the court makes an order.[247] However, there remains a right for the removed contract-holder to apply back to the court for the next six months to have the original order rescinded.[248]

In circumstances where a landlord believes that a joint contract-holder has carried out anti-social behaviour they can also serve notice in the relevant prescribed form[249] and then apply to the court to have them, and only them, removed from the contract. Notice must also be given to all other contract-holders in a prescribed form.[250] The court application can be made immediately on service of the notice but must be made within six months. The court may make an order for possession against the joint contract-holder only if they would have made the same order had that contract-holder been a sole contract-holder.

Joint contract-holders may also withdraw from contracts. No joint contract-holder may unilaterally end any form of occupation contract.[251] This essentially overturns the existing case law on notice by joint tenants[252] and removes the distinction in that case-law between fixed-

---

[246] Form RHW31.

[247] RHWA, s227.

[248] RHWA, s228.

[249] Form RHW32.

[250] Form RHW33.

[251] RHWA, s231.

[252] *Hammersmith & Fulham LBC v Monk* [1991] UKHL 6

term and periodic contracts. However, a joint contract-holder under a periodic contract is entitled to withdraw from that contract by giving a withdrawal notice to the landlord. The joint contract-holder must warn all other joint contract-holders of their intent to withdraw in writing and the landlord must do so as well. On the expiry of that notice the contract will end for that contract-holder.[253]

---

[253] RHWA, s130.

CHAPTER TEN

ABANDONMENT

The RHWA makes detailed provision for the abandonment of premises.[254] The operation of these provisions is not dissimilar to those passed by Parliament in England but never brought into force.[255] The RHWA provisions only apply to premises where the occupation contract contains a provision specifying that the occupier may only occupy that premises as their only or principal home.

The RHWA sets out a clear process for situations where a landlord believes that a property has been abandoned.[256] The landlord must give the contract holder a notice of intention to terminate the tenancy for suspected abandonment. There is a form prescribed for this purpose.[257] The form must notify the contract-holder that the landlord believes they have abandoned the property, that they must tell the landlord in writing within four weeks if the landlord is wrong, and that the landlord will end the contract if they do not hear from the contract-holder. At the end of the four-week period the landlord can serve notice using a further prescribed form[258] and the contract will end. At that time the landlord is entitled to recover possession without going to court. Copies of the relevant notices must be given to lodgers or anyone with a sub-contract under the primary contract.

---

[254] In Chapter 13, Part 9.

[255] See Part 3, Housing and Planning Act 2016.

[256] Section 220, RHWA.

[257] Form RHW27.

[258] Form RHW28.

The abandonment process in the RHWA owes a great deal to similar provisions found in English legislation.[259] However, the English provisions have never been brought into force and so the RHWA has effectively overtaken these provisions.

Abandoned Possessions

It does depend on the manner in which possession is granted. The Act is silent on this issue where possession is being granted in accordance with one of the rights to possession through the courts. The supplementary provisions applicable to tenancies under the RHWA require that a contract-holder removes all their property at the end of their occupation contract.[260] If they fail to do so when possession has been awarded the traditional position under the Torts (Interference with Goods) Act will presumably apply.

If the tenant has abandoned the property then there are abandonment provisions in the RHWA.[261] Where these have been utilised by a landlord then there is a power, which has been utilised, to make regulations to deal with the delivery or disposal of that property by the landlord.[262] Those regulations specify that any property must be retained for four weeks from the day the landlord recovers his premises before disposal or sale. There is an exemption which does not require property to be retained if it:

- Is perishable so it will not last the four weeks;

---

[259] Part 3, Housing and Planning Act 2016

[260] Regulation 8 of the Renting Homes (Supplementary Provisions) (Wales) Regulations 2022.

[261] S220, RHWA.

[262] S221, RHWA and the Renting Homes (Safeguarding Property in Abandoned Dwellings) (Wales) Regulations 2022.

- Is of a type which will require costly or inconvenient storage. Freezer contents would fall into this category;

- Is of such a low value that the cost of storing it for the period will exceed its value.

At the end of the four-week period the landlord may sell or dispose of the property and may apply any sum realised by that sale to his reasonable storage costs. Any monies remaining after that can be applied against rent arrears. At any stage during the four-week period the contract holder or anyone who appears to actually own the property may seek for it to be returned to them. The landlord is not obliged to make arrangements to deliver those items but merely make them available for collection. Landlords may also insist on being paid storage costs incurred, but not other sums owed to them, as a condition of handing over the property.

In practice, this structure is likely to be highly beneficial to landlords whose occupiers abandon their property. Most occupiers leave nothing of substantial value when they abandon a property and so it is likely to be uncommon that those items will exceed the cost of storage for the required four-week period. The value of white goods and other consumer electronics and appliances of uncertain provenance that have been abandoned is very low and the cost of storage is likely to exceed their value.

However, the existing legislation dealing with abandoned possessions has not been modified or repealed for Wales by the RHWA.[263] So it is unclear how these new RHWA provisions will interact with that legislation.

---

[263] Torts (Interference with Goods) Act 1977.

CHAPTER ELEVEN

THE RHWA AND
THE COURTS

The courts have also had to change their rules[264] in order to accommodate the RHWA. The main changes are to the rules on possession[265] and the rules on miscellaneous claims about land.[266]

RHWA claims are claims that do not relate to possession, prohibited conduct standard contract orders, or disrepair.[267] These are ordinarily to be made in the County Court other than in exceptional circumstances when they can be started in the High Court.[268] If the claim is to be started in the High Court then it must be started in the Chancery Division.[269] If a claim is started inappropriately in the High Court then the High Court may strike it out or transfer it back to the County Court.[270] Generally, the rule relating to matters involving land that can be started in the County Court is that this is almost always the appropriate venue as there is a very high bar for starting claims in the High Court. No forms for this claim type appear to have been specified at the time of writing but the claim form must set out:

---

[264] By way of the Civil Procedure (Amendment No. 2) Rules 2022 and the 149th Practice Direction Update.

[265] Civil Procedure Rules, Part 55.

[266] Civil Procedure Rules, Part 56 and new Practice Direction 56A.

[267] Civil Procedure Rules, Part 56.5(b).

[268] Practice Direction 56A, para 2.2.

[269] Practice Direction 56A, para 2.8.

[270] Practice Direction 56A, para 2.3.

- the dwelling to which the claim relates;

- the particulars of the current occupation contract including the date, parties and term;

- any notices relevant to the claim;

- the specific provisions of the RHWA under which the claim is being brought.

Different types of claim require other information to be given but in general where there is a notice being appealed then details of that notice must be given, and where there is an appeal against a decision or refusal to consent then details of that decision or refusal must be given.

There is no clear statement as to whether the claims are part 7 or part 8 claims but as many claims under the rules on miscellaneous claims about land are made as part 8 claims then it seems likely that most of the RHWA claims will be part 8 claims. However, claims seeking compensation for landlord or tenant breaches or deposit protection failings are explicitly required to be part 7 claims.[271]

It remains to be seen how RHWA claims will be dealt with in practice. Wales has a small judiciary and a an even smaller number of judges sitting at circuit level and above. It may be that appeals from District Judges will be heard by a Circuit Judge sitting as a Deputy High Court Judge. This would have the benefit of giving a clear and binding ruling on a point heard by that judge and therefore provide more certainty. The other option is for District Judges to give permission to appeal and assign that appeal direct to the Court of Appeal on the basis that there is an "important point of principle or practice" which would directly benefit from the input of the Court of Appeal.[272] The first option is likely to hear

---

[271] Practice Direction 56A, para 4.7, 4.9 & 4.13.

[272] Under Civil Procedure Rule, 52.23.

more cases more quickly while the second would give a far more authoritative solution. In practice, it is likely that both options will be used.

CHAPTER TWELVE

CONCLUSION

The RHWA is likely to end up being one of the most substantial re-boots of landlord and tenant law for a generation. While Scotland and Northern Ireland have also made changes and England has sought to tweak aspect so its legislation, Wales is looking at a complete revision of both the private and social sectors with a totally new way of thinking. While the final version of the RHWA is not as ambitious as the original proposals from the Law Commission, it remains a radical proposition which seeks to erode the separation between social and private sector occupations and also the difference between tenancies and licences in the residential sector.

While the RHWA is complex it is likely that familiarity will lead to some of the confusion that surrounds it reducing over time. That said there are real questions as to whether the new regime will truly alter the relationship between landlords and their occupiers or simply move the conflicts and power relationships that exist onto a different track. The fact that the RHWA has led to long and complex written agreements is not a good sign in terms of promoting occupier understanding and its potentially heavy use of the courts is likely to be a problem in terms of occupiers actually obtaining the rights the RHWA seeks to give them.

Whatever happens, the RHWA is a fact of life in residential housing in Wales. How it proceeds from here depends on how the altered relationships it creates between landlords, agents, and occupiers proceed and how the courts elect to interpret the law.

APPENDIX ONE

LIST OF RHWA FORMS
AND THEIR PURPOSE

The forms below are prescribed in regulations.[273] Where a form is prescribed the RHWA states that where a notice is not in the prescribed form then it is of no effect unless regulations say otherwise.[274] However, the forms regulations also state that a "form substantially to the same effect as the prescribed form is valid".[275] This is clearly intended to be an expression of the existing case law on this issue in relation to notices under residential tenancies.[276] This states that a notice is substantially to the same effect if "notwithstanding errors or omissions" it accomplishes the statutory requirement when read by a reasonable recipient in the appropriate context.

Form Number	Form Title	Purpose
RHW1	Notice of standard contract	Form used by a community landlord where they intend to offer a standard as opposed to a secure contract

---

[273] The Renting Homes (Prescribed Forms) (Wales) Regulations 2022.

[274] RHWA, s236(3).

[275] Regulation 3(2), the Renting Homes (Prescribed Forms) (Wales) Regulations 2022.

[276] *Ravenseft Properties Ltd v Hall* [2001] EWCA Civ 2034.

RHW2	Notice of landlord's address	Form required by s39(1) to inform contract-holder of landlord's address
RHW3	Change of landlord's identity and notice of new landlord's address	Form required by s39(2) to inform contract-holder of a new landlord and their address
RHW4	Change in landlord's address	Form required by s39(3) to inform contract-holder of landlord's new address
RHW5	Conditions imposed by head landlord when consenting to a sub-occupation contract	Form required by s61(2) where a superior landlord is agreeing to a sub-contract but is doing so only with conditions being imposed
RHW6	Head landlord's decision to treat sub-occupation contract as a periodic standard contract	Form required by s61(7) where a superior landlord consented to a sub-contract with conditions which were not complied with and the head landlord elects to treat the sub-contract as a periodic standard contract
RHW7	Notice to sub-holder of a possession claim against the contract holder	Form required by s64(2) where a superior landlord has allowed a sub-contract to be entered into and then gives notice to the intermediate contract-holder

RHW8	Extended possession claim against the sub-holder	Form required by s65(3) where a superior landlord has allowed a sub-contract to be entered into and then makes a possession claim against the intermediate contract-holder where they also intend to seek possession against the sub-holder
RHW9	Notice of potential exclusion of contract-holder after abandoning the head contract and the sub-occupation contract	Notice given by a contract-holder under s66(4) who is occupying under a sub-contract where he believes his immediate landlord has abandoned the sub-contract and the superior contract
RHW10	Transfer of an occupation contract by a contract-holder	Notice under s69(1)(a) where a contract-holder wishes to transfer their contract to another party
RHW11	Transfer of rights and obligations under an occupation contract by a joint contract-holder	Form for a joint contract-holder to transfer their rights and obligations to another party under s69(1)(b)
RHW12	Notice of variation of rent	Notice under s104 or s123 to vary the rent
RHW13	Transfer of rights and obligations under a fixed term standard contract by a joint contract-holder	Form for a sole contract-holder to transfer their rights and obligations to another party under s69(1)(a)

RHW14	Transfer of rights and obligations under a fixed term standard contract on the death of a joint contract-holder	Form for a joint contract-holder to tell other contract-holders that their rights and obligations to another party on death under s142(2)
RHW15	Notice of temporary exclusion (Supported Standard Contract)	Notice under s145 of exclusion in a supported standard contract
RHW16	Notice of termination – Periodic Standard Contract with six-month minimum notice period (other than Introductory Standard Contract or Prohibited Conduct Standard Contract)	Notice to end a periodic standard contract without specific cause where six month's notice is required
RHW17	Notice of termination – Periodic Standard Contract with two-month minimum notice period (other than Introductory Standard Contract or Prohibited Conduct Standard Contract)	Notice to end a periodic standard contract without specific cause where only two month's notice is required due to a Schedule 8A exclusion

RHW18	Notice of termination – introductory standard contract or prohibited conduct standard contract	Termination notices specifically for introductory or prohibited conduct standard contracts
RHW19	Withdrawal of landlord's notice of termination – Periodic Standard Contract	Form for landlords to use where they wish to withdraw a termination notice under s180(3)
RHW20	Possession claim on the ground of serious rent arrears – Standard Contract (other than Introductory Standard Contract or Prohibited Conduct Standard Contract)	Notice for landlord to seek to terminate a standard contract for serious rent arrears under s181 or s187
RHW21	Possession claim on the grounds of serious rent arrears – Introductory Standard Contract or Prohibited Conduct Standard Contract	Notice for landlord to seek to terminate an introductory or prohibited conduct standard contract for serious rent arrears under s181
RHW22	Notice of termination – Fixed Term Standard Contract within	Notice for landlords who wish to terminate a fixed term standard contract at the end of that fixed

	Schedule 9B to the Renting Homes (Wales) Act 2016	term under s186 where that contract falls within Schedule 9B
RHW23	Notice before making a possession claim	Form to give notice for claims for possession based on breaches of contract or estate management grounds
RHW24	Notice of termination under landlord's break clause – fixed term standard contract with six-month minimum notice period	Notice to end a fixed term standard contract without specific cause in reliance on a break clause under s194 where six month's notice is required
RHW25	Notice of termination under landlord's break clause – fixed term standard contract with two-month minimum notice period	Notice to end a fixed term standard contract without specific cause in reliance on a break clause under s194 where two month's notice is required under Schedule 8A
RHW26	Withdrawal of notice of termination under landlord's break clause – fixed term standard contract	Form for landlords to use where they wish to withdraw a termination notice given in respect of a break clause under s201(3)

RHW27	Landlord's intention to end occupation contract due to abandonment	Form to give notice of the intent to end the contract for abandonment under s220
RHW28	End of occupation contract due to abandonment	Form to end the contract for abandonment under s220
RHW29	Landlord's intention to end rights and obligations of a joint contract-holder due to non-occupation	Form for a landlord to tell a joint contract-holder that they intend to end their rights and obligations under the contract are ending as the joint contract-holder does not occupy or intend to occupy the property under s225(3)
RHW30	End of rights and obligations of a joint contract-holder due to non-occupation	Form for a landlord to actually end the rights and obligations of a joint contract-holder on the basis that the joint contract-holder does not occupy or intend to occupy the property under s225(3)
RHW31	Notice of joint contract-holder's intention to apply for an order ending rights and obligations of another joint contract-holder due to non-occupation	Form for a joint contract-holder to tell another contract-holder that they will be applying to the court under s227(3) for an order to end that contract-holders rights and obligations on the basis that they are not or do not intend to occupy the property

RHW32	Landlord's intention to apply for an order ending a joint contract-holder's rights and obligations due to prohibited conduct	Form for a landlord to notify a joint contract-holder of their intention to apply to the court under s230(2) to end their occupation contract for prohibited conduct
RHW33	Notice to other joint contract-holders of landlord's intention to apply for an order ending a joint contract-holders rights and obligations due to prohibited conduct	Form for a landlord to notify joint contract-holders of the landlord's intention to apply to the court under s230(2) to end the occupation contract of another joint contract-holder for prohibited conduct
RHW34	Extension of introductory period	Form to notify a contract-holder that their introductory period is to be extended under Schedule 4, para 3
RHW35	Intention to apply for an order imposing a Prohibited Conduct Standard Contract	Form to notify a contract-holder of the landlord's intention to ask the court to impose a prohibited conduct standard contract under Schedule 7, para 1
RHW36	End of probation period – Prohibited Conduct Standard Contract	Form to notify the contract-holder of the ending of their prohibited conduct standard contract probation period under Schedule 7, para 3

| RHW37 | Extension of probation period (Prohibited Conduct Standard Contract) | Form to notify the contract-holder of the extending of their prohibited conduct standard contract probation period under Schedule 7, para 4 |
| RHW38 | Notice of termination – Fixed Term Standard Contract (Converted Contract) | Form for terminating Assured Shorthold Tenancies for a fixed term that have become RHWA contracts where notice can be given for termination at the end of the fixed term under Schedule 12, para 25B. |

APPENDIX TWO

LIST OF REGULATIONS
MADE UNDER THE RHWA

The Renting Homes (Supplementary Provisions) (Wales) Regulations 2022

The Renting Homes (Supported Standard Contracts) (Supplementary Provisions) (Wales) Regulations 2022

The Renting Homes (Model Written Statements of Contract) (Wales) Regulations 2022

The Renting Homes (Explanatory Information for Written Statements of Occupation Contracts) (Wales) Regulations 2022

The Renting Homes (Fitness for Human Habitation) (Wales) Regulations 2022

The Renting Homes (Wales) Act 2016 (Amendment of Schedule 9A) Regulations 2022

The Renting Homes (Safeguarding Property in Abandoned Dwellings) (Wales) Regulations 2022

The Renting Homes (Review of Decisions) (Wales) Regulations 2022

The Renting Homes (Deposit Schemes) (Required Information) (Wales) Regulations 2022

The Renting Homes (Prescribed Forms) (Wales) Regulations 2022

The Renting Homes (Wales) Act 2016 (Consequential Amendments) Regulations 2022

The Renting Homes (Wales) Act 2016 (Amendment) Regulations 2022

Renting Homes (Rent Determination) (Converted Contracts) (Wales) Regulations 2022

The Renting Homes (Wales) Act 2016 (Amendment of Schedule 12) Regulations 2022

The Renting Homes (Wales) Act 2016 (Housing Association Tenancies: Fundamental Provisions) Regulations 2022

The Renting Homes (Wales) Act 2016 (Saving and Transitional Provisions) Regulations 2022

The Renting Homes (Wales) Act 2016 (Consequential Amendments to Secondary Legislation) Regulations 2022

The Renting Homes (Wales) Act 2016 (Commencement No. 2 and Consequential Amendments) Order 2022

Renting Homes (Amendment) (Wales) Act 2021 (Commencement) Order 2022

The Renting Homes (Rent Determination) (Converted Contracts) (Wales) (Amendment) Regulations 2022

The Renting Homes (Wales) Act 2016 (Consequential Amendments to Secondary Legislation) (Amendment) Regulations 2022

The Renting Homes (Fitness for Human Habitation) (Amendment) (Wales) Regulations 2022

The Renting Homes (Wales) Act 2016 (Amendment of Schedule 12 and Consequential Amendment) Regulations 2022

MORE BOOKS BY
LAW BRIEF PUBLISHING

A selection of our other titles available now:-

'A Practical Guide to Parental Alienation in Private and Public Law Children Cases' by Sam King QC & Frankie Shama
'Contested Heritage – Removing Art from Land and Historic Buildings' by Richard Harwood QC, Catherine Dobson, David Sawtell
'The Limits of Separate Legal Personality: When Those Running a Company Can Be Held Personally Liable for Losses Caused to Third Parties Outside of the Company' by Dr Mike Wilkinson
'A Practical Guide to Transgender Law' by Robin Moira White & Nicola Newbegin
'Artificial Intelligence – The Practical Legal Issues (2nd Edition)' by John Buyers
'A Practical Guide to Residential Freehold Conveyancing' by Lorraine Richardson
'A Practical Guide to Pensions on Divorce for Lawyers' by Bryan Scant
'A Practical Guide to Challenging Sham Marriage Allegations in Immigration Law' by Priya Solanki
'A Practical Guide to Legal Rights in Scotland' by Sarah-Jane Macdonald
'A Practical Guide to New Build Conveyancing' by Paul Sams & Rebecca East
'A Practical Guide to Defending Barristers in Disciplinary Cases' by Marc Beaumont
'A Practical Guide to Inherited Wealth on Divorce' by Hayley Trim
'A Practical Guide to Practice Direction 12J and Domestic Abuse in Private Law Children Proceedings' by Rebecca Cross & Malvika Jaganmohan
'A Practical Guide to Confiscation and Restraint' by Narita Bahra QC, John Carl Townsend, David Winch
'A Practical Guide to the Law of Forests in Scotland' by Philip Buchan
'A Practical Guide to Health and Medical Cases in Immigration Law' by Rebecca Chapman & Miranda Butler
'A Practical Guide to Bad Character Evidence for Criminal Practitioners by Aparna Rao
'A Practical Guide to Extradition Law post-Brexit' by Myles Grandison et al

These books and more are available to order online direct from the publisher at www.lawbriefpublishing.com, where you can also read free sample chapters. For any queries, contact us on 0844 587 2383 or mail@lawbriefpublishing.com.

Our books are also usually in stock at www.amazon.co.uk with free next day delivery for Prime members, and at good legal bookshops such as Wildy & Sons.

We are regularly launching new books in our series of practical day-to-day practitioners' guides. Visit our website and join our free newsletter to be kept informed and to receive special offers, free chapters, etc.

You can also follow us on Twitter at www.twitter.com/lawbriefpub.